UNIVERSAL AUTHORITY

The Politics and Religion of Space
Exploration and Time Travel

James Grey

iUniverse, Inc.
Bloomington

Universal Authority
The Politics and Religion of Space Exploration and Time Travel

Copyright © 2011 James Grey

iUniverse books may be ordered through booksellers or by contacting:

iUniverse
1663 Liberty Drive
Bloomington, IN 47403
www.iuniverse.com
1-800-Authors (1-800-288-4677)

ISBN: 978-1-4620-3356-0 (sc)
ISBN: 978-1-4620-3357-7 (e)

Printed in the United States of America

iUniverse rev. date: 7/7/2011

Dedications

I would like to dedicate this work to
the memory of my parents

Stanley Clinton Grey
31 May 1935 – 2 October 1979

Marie Jane Dinsmore Grey
24 October 1935 – 15 November 2010

"It is precisely because I believe theologically that there is a being called God, and that he is infinite in intelligence, freedom, and power, that I cannot take it upon myself *to limit what he might have done.*"
Father Theodore M. Hesburgh

"Do not pray for tasks equal to your powers, pray for powers equal to your tasks."
Phillip Brooks

Contents

Foreword   xi
Introduction   xxi

Part 1

Space Exploration and
Extra-Terrestrial Research 1

Part 2

Science, Physics and
Time Travel   35

Conclusion   69
Acknowledgements   75
References   77

Foreword

In the living room of my home growing up there was a painting of President John F. Kennedy. The one thing I remember about this particular masterpiece was that no matter which direction you moved the eyes would follow you, a remarkable work of art by the painter but none the less frightening to a six year old child who had been taught since birth that ghosts and boogers loomed around every corner.

I assume that every child is told at some point or another that if they misbehave the booger man will come to visit. He will never come in the waking hours of the well lit day time so that he can enjoy a cup of coffee while you are able to debrief him about whom and what he really is and assist him in learning his true calling.

I am thankful for my Mother's eventual honesty when she told me the truth concerning the raging madness of those who make their living in the world of art (an occupation for which I hold the deepest respect), and her next statement whether or not correct is what lay the foundation for everything I would pursue over the course of my life.

My Mother told me emphatically that upon the passing of my Father, God had given me John F. Kennedy as a surrogate Father and that if I would study his life and accomplishments I would go far no matter what direction I moved in.

I never understood for some time why she simply did not tell me to follow the example of my own Father, however as time went on I came to comprehend the difference between Kennedy's marvelous speeches and my Father's drunken rages.

I was six years old when my Father passed away as the result of a massive heart attack. I can remember 2 October 1979, as if it were last week.

I was in the first grade at Greendale Elementary School in Abingdon, Virginia when my Mother walked into the classroom visibly shaken.

I cannot deny that this scene made me somewhat uneasy and as she made her way passed me to the teacher I asked her what was wrong. The only response I received was the words "Daddy Died". That one statement truly changed my life forever.

I loved my Father and losing him in that way left me with emptiness that words cannot express, yet life goes on with or without the ones we love.

I cannot remember every single place we lived however we had relocated our residence seventeen times prior to my Father's passing. The reason for this was my Father's absolute refusal to relinquish the rent money on time or in many cases at all.

I loved my Father and I know that he loved me, however when you have an addiction to a substance, especially alcohol you are drawn to put that substance ahead of those you love the most. I do not harbor any resentment whatsoever and I only wish there was some way to let him know that.

I am thankful for the kindness of the land owner on whose property we lived at the time for allowing my Mother and me to remain there for twenty dollars per month.

The house sat right on the side of the road, was structured with wood and covered with brick siding. In the event you have never observed this substance it is similar to tar paper and has the appearance of brick.

I was your typical child who was never satisfied with anything and the fact that our house did not have running water became a burr in my saddle which had me constantly raring back snorting and exhorting my emotions.

I have heard that there is a silver lining behind every cloud and the fact that we had a creek directly across the road must have been that silver lining.

I used two metal pails to acquire water for bathing and laundry while drinking water came from generous neighbors and was stored in empty milk containers my Mother reserved for that purpose.

I am sure that some people recall outhouses and we had several of them over the twelve year period we lived there.

I will never forget the last one we had constructed, a neighbor friend and I dug the hole. Following a short discussion about how long and wide it should be we finally decided that the measurements should be as long and wide as the length of the shovel. I guarantee the final results were at least ten feet four square.

The completed structure served its designed purpose as well as that of storage shed. I covered the floor in linoleum and on occasion used it as a bath house.

The winters here in Southwest Virginia can be bitter cold and heat bills can soar. The sweet thing looking back is that we burned wood and coal.

I hated going outside to the coal pile and carrying coal into the house; wood was even worse as I frequently acquired splinters with nearly every armful I bore.

I liked school in one way and in another way I hated it. I may as well admit what the teachers already knew and that is the fact that no matter what I learned it always took me twice as long as anyone else. I am what they call a slow learner.

I was retained in the first grade for several reasons among

which were my inability to read and write. I learned these necessities the following year with the help of special teachers in a class with only a few students.

I learned slowly yet surely and in the second grade I was reading on a higher level than the other students. I never had any trouble with reading and writing from that point on but struggled with math all the way through school.

I passed the second and third grades easily but the fourth grade proved to be a turning point, metaphorically everyone else was turning while I was as stationary as a rock. The entire curriculum changed and I felt like Jed Clampet in a Harvard Philosophy class. I was unable to retain the required material so therefore I was retained.

I repeated the fourth grade and again found myself in those special classes with only a few students. I was not totally offended because of my ability to read and write faster than the rest of the class and used this to elevate my confidence level. I was in my own way of thinking, the smartest child in the school.

I passed the second year and moved on to the fifth grade. Like an explorer lost in the jungle with nothing but hope and a prayer, I somehow managed to make my way through the metaphoric growth and poisonous vipers of reading, writing, arithmetic and the occasional science to emerge into the sunlight of Grade School completion.

I started Abingdon High School in the fall of 1988 and that is where my real education was acquired.

I had grown up in a Caucasian environment with the only exceptions being my fifth grade teacher and the barber who cut my hair. I thought the world of both, still do and would fight to defend either one.

I admit that I had a fear of African Americans, due in part to misrepresentations over the years, however; as I became acquainted with the student body I realized that the black students were in a lot of ways friendlier and more pleasant to associate with than many of my fellow Caucasians.

I was never much of an athlete however I managed to run track and field in the eighth, ninth and tenth grades throwing the shot-put and discuss. Though I did not throw them for a great distance I can say that my name appears on all of the old rosters for those track meets.

I passed everything until the tenth grade when I made the decision that I was going to be an academic golden child.

I enrolled in several college preparatory courses as well as Spanish One. I failed both English and Spanish in the same year and could make no claim other than I was speechless.

I will never forget the evening of 17 May 1991 when our neighbor picked me up at school and announced that our house had been destroyed by fire. I cannot explain the feelings and emotions which overtook me despite her first statement being that Mom was alright.

The fire trucks were lined up both above and below the house with concerned neighbors and friends coming from all directions. I believe that our pastor had already arrived and was conversing with my Mother who was sitting in someone's car.

I exited the vehicle in which I was riding and walked over to Mom in order to comfort her as I could tell that she was emotionally distraught.

I am unable to express verbally how it feels to stand and see everything you have go up in smoke.

I became a Born-Again Christian in the living room of that house which I often refer to as the old home place.

My Mother and I found ourselves staying in the homes of friends and neighbors, a practice with which I was never comfortable even in times of financial strength and ease.

I will assert here that one of the greatest blessings in my life has been a Church Family who has been there for my Mother and me on more than one occasion.

The community came together with donations of food, clothing and money while our Church Family worked tirelessly to purchase and set up a single wide trailer on the site of the old home place.

I am not sure who stepped forward and paid the rent on a small nearby house where we lived for the next two months but they know who they are and their generosity was and still is appreciated.

I cannot recall the exact date but about two months later in July 1991 my Mother and I moved into a brand new mobile home. The Church put the trailer in Mom's name and presented her with the title.

The property on which the house and now trailer sat, by this time had been purchased by a family friend. My Mother and I continued to live there in exchange for upkeep.

I was overjoyed to finally live in a dwelling with indoor plumbing and electric heat. I say that of course because I was not paying and never even saw the electric bill.

I thought for certain that my life had truly changed for the better. I was planning what I would do after high school and then on the evening of 6 March 1992 my world was turned upside down.

I had arrived home from school and as usual I had the house to myself. Mom was healthcare provider for an elderly lady with whom we had attended church and whose son owned the property we lived on. Mom never got home until about two hours after I did.

The telephone rang and upon answering it I recognized the voice of the daughter of Mom's client.

I sat there at the kitchen table as she explained to me how my Mother had suffered a stroke and was in the hospital.

In about one hour I was standing beside of a hospital bed looking at my semi-conscious Mother who was hooked up to several machines. Mom had a look of fear on her face which

I had never seen before. I was absolutely numb with fear and disbelief.

I believe the hospital stay was about two weeks and then Mom was assigned to a local Skilled Nursing Facility where she remained for an entire month while receiving therapy in order to rebuild her strength.

Mom returned home with several issues, among which was her diabetes. Insulin was required in order to control her blood sugar level and the high dosages sometimes caused it to drop low.

I was relieved that Mom could administer her own injections even though she was unable to prepare them. I still felt uneasy leaving her alone and worried constantly.

I spent my final two years of high school studying Automobile Mechanics. I had only one dream and one goal at that time and that was to race NASCAR.

I was convinced that if I learned how to build and rebuild engines I could acquire employment in that very industry. I may well have been able to, had I known at that time how to organize my priorities and have taken the curriculum a little more seriously.

There were several students and teachers who had race cars in the class and I utilized a majority of my time sitting in them looking at magazines.

I graduated Abingdon High School on 9 June 1993 and went directly into the work force. I performed odd jobs and temporary labor with brief intermissions until September 1994 when I was hired by Shoney's of Abingdon first as a cook and then as a dishwasher and busboy.

I remained there for four and one half years before accepting employment in the Private Property Protection Industry as an Unarmed Security Officer, in which capacity I remain.

I became involved in the political process in 1995 and remained involved through 2001 running unsuccessfully for local office and assisting the efforts of more than one party.

I have steered clear of the political process and public eye for the last ten years and do not have any regrets.

I am not saying that I will remain neutral for the rest of my life as there are issues worth fighting for and as opinionated as I am there is always the possibility of an uprising.

In 2009 I felt that the Almighty was calling me to increase my qualifications. I sought ordination as a minister through the web page of the Universal Life Church in Modesto, California and received it on 27 April of that year.

I do not pastor a congregation and do not feel led in that direction. I feel that God wanted me to receive ordination for the purpose of credentials and that he would direct my steps along the way.

I have but one goal and that is to minister the gospel to as many people as possible before the second coming of Jesus Christ, *commonly referred to as the rapture.*

The Bible clearly states that no man knows the day or the hour that this event will take place so therefore we as Christians do not need to be wasting any time in revealing his word.

I experienced the final blow that life could deal to me on 15 November 2010 when my Mother passed away as the result of congestive heart failure at the age of seventy-five years.

I was saddened yet relieved that she was no longer suffering as she had been confined to a Skilled Nursing Facility for the past three years due to loss of mobility and blood cancer.

I devoted my time to caring for the woman who cared for me since I was six years old. I never saw my Mother as a burden but felt an obligation to her and could not stop thinking that I owed a debt that no amount of money could ever repay.

I immediately moved out of Mom's mobile home and sold it to a family friend. I was happy to finally be released from the responsibility of keeping up the land on which I had lived since the age of five.

There are people who for sentimental reasons do not want

to part with property that has been in their family for years but I am not one of them.

I am comfortable in my current apartment residence as I work forty hours per week and write in my spare time.

Introduction

I became interested in the subjects of Extra-Terrestrial Research and Time Travel in December 2004. I cannot recall exactly what it was that manifested that interest, perhaps it was something I saw on television, heard on radio or read in a magazine, book or some other publication.

I wanted to study them in depth and learn as much as possible about their past, present and future. I directed my studies in the areas of science, physics and theology as opposed to immersing myself in science fiction stories despite the fact that I enjoy good entertainment.

I was excited to find as much literary material and positive discussion with regard to these issues as I did. The only negative feelings that overtook me were related to the fact someone was ahead of me in the quest to meet our neighbors and travel in time.

I realize that there will always be a cloud of suspicion over these and other subjects considered by many to be fantasy as opposed to reality. The controversy however, is what appeals to me and drives me to literary expression.

I encounter quite a bit of resistance when attempting to discuss these issues with other people. I find that even those who believe in Intelligent Extra-Terrestrial Existence and Time Travel possess opinions which conflict with my own.

I do the best I can to recall the questions people pose and then I search for ways to answer those questions to the benefit of my argument.

There is one thing that I have discovered through my conversations and that is the fact that every discussion falls into one of three categories; Scientific, Legal or Religious.

The earth has a scientific makeup. Atoms and molecules as well as other particles comprised together each have a specific job just as individuals on an assembly line. In the event one particle fails to pull its weight the results can be cancerous.

The earth with no one on it would cancel the need for the second category which is legal. The earth has people on it so therefore in order to live peacefully with one another it is necessary that we have laws by which we live and engage one another; otherwise there would be complete chaos.

Religious is the most powerful of the three because it invokes the most emotion in people. The foreign governments with which America is currently at war have legal systems that are set up based on their holy books and the manifestos of their founders.

In addressing issues like Extra-Terrestrial Intelligence and Time Travel all three categories must be touched on otherwise they will make their way into the discussion on their own.

There has to be scientific proof as to whether or not something exists even if that proof is simple eyewitness accounts.

There are legal questions surrounding the issues because of territorial rights. In the event an Extra-Terrestrial race were to visit earth what would be their limits while living among us?

If someone were to travel in time whether backward or forward what would be their legal obligations?

In the event they were at Ford's Theatre on 14 April 1865 would they become an accessory to President Lincoln's assassination by not providing the President or some member of his security detail with information as to what was about to happen?

If they were to travel forward and see some great catastrophe would they be obligated to inform those who were to be affected? Would the accessory clause apply in the event they did not surrender information?

The only argument that would be of assistance in court is that interference with time would create paradoxes and ripple effects which could be felt for years to come.

The religious argument concerning Extra-Terrestrial Intelligence is that if there is an intelligent race somewhere other than earth then who is their Savior? Adam and Eve were the first two humans and the Bible records history from the Garden of Eden through Revelation without mention of God's love for any other race than human.

The religious argument concerning time travel is that if time began as it is recorded in Genesis and will end as it is recorded in Revelation then time must be a straight line. Can we move back and forth on that line?

I have an interest in science as a Christian and creationist. When God created the heavens and the earth he did so by intelligent design. I also have an interest in mechanics, the different parts of an engine work together in a specific order bringing about an overall result which is an operational automobile, yet the engine did not evolve it had an inventor.

I grew up admiring the legacies of President Kennedy and his brother Robert, as well as Dr. Martin Luther King, Jr. I am of a certainty interested in and hold a respect for the legal aspect of all things.

I grew up in a Christian home where the Bible was accepted as the complete word of Almighty God without error. I have never departed from my up bringing and do not have any plans to do so. I may find myself at odds with other Christians on certain issues and remain unwilling to budge; however, I seek to prove my point or at least provide detailed and sensible argument which will cause them to either stutter or pause on or before answers.

There is one thing that no one can deny and that is the fact that God is Almighty, all powerful and all knowing. God knows exactly what will happen before it happens and whether or not he will interfere is entirely up to him.

Nothing happens unless God allows it to. If we sense an immediate danger and get to safety right at the last minute we may see it as divine intervention when it is in reality part of the original plan.

I do not provide this work to cause people to believe in something they do not already believe in. I provide it for those who do believe and for the purpose of causing them to consider the fact of one intelligent creator. A Creator who may not have exposed us to his entire masterpiece or may not have exposed them to us, I'm not sure which way it goes.

I ask of you one favor and that is to read and consider this work before you dismiss it. I realize that it is controversial and will draw criticism from many who do not agree with my beliefs and interpretations; however, it is an act of labor and love for those, who like me, do not limit God's creative freedom. I am reaching out and inviting them to study, accept and know our Creator in a personal way.

"Come now, and let us reason together, saith the Lord: though your sins be as scarlet, they shall be as white as snow; though they be red like crimson, they shall be as wool".
Isaiah 1:18
KJV 1611

PART 1

SPACE EXPLORATION AND EXTRA-TERRESTRIAL RESEARCH

Space Exploration and Extra-Terrestrial Research

*"Its not the hours you put into your work,
its work you put in your hours"
-Sam Ewing*

The above referenced statement truly defines the United States efforts and accomplishments in Space Exploration and Extra-Terrestrial research.

According to Wikipedia, "NASA is an executive branch of the United States Government, responsible for the nation's civilian space program and aeronautics and aerospace research".

NASA went into full effect on 1 October 1958. The creation of NASA was related to the pressures of National Defense.

The Soviet Union launched Sputnik One, the world's first artificial satellite as its IGY entry on 4 October 1957.

The launch of Sputnik One gave the illusion of a technological gap between the United States and a country responsible for American unrest.

This illusion provided the United States with good reason to increase spending in space exploration. America set out to be the front runner in aerospace endeavors, technical and scientific educational programs and the chartering of new federal agencies to manage air and space research and development.

NASA'S first high-profile program involving human spaceflight was Project Mercury. Project Mercury was an effort to learn whether or not human beings could survive the rigors of spaceflight.

Alan B. Shepard, Jr. became the first American to fly into space when he rode his mercury capsule on a 15-minute suborbital mission. This feat was accomplished on 5 May 1961.

John H. Glenn became the first U.S. astronaut to orbit the earth on 2 February 1962. Project Mercury performed six flights achieving its goal of putting piloted spacecraft into earth orbit and retrieving the astronauts safely.

The next big endeavor was Project Gemini which built on Mercury's accomplishments and extended NASA'S manned spaceflight program to spacecraft designed for two astronauts.

Project Gemini performed a total of ten flights providing NASA'S engineers with more data on weightlessness, perfected reentry and splashdown procedures and demonstrated rendezvous and docking in space.

Project Gemini experienced one of its many highlights on 3 June 1965 during mission four when Edward H. White, Jr. became the first U.S. astronaut to conduct a space walk.

Projects Mercury and Gemini were extremely beneficial to the American Space Exploration program. Mercury and Gemini provided valuable data which would assist NASA in future endeavors including Project Apollo.

Project Apollo was the largest investment made by the United States in Space Exploration. The total cost over the life of the program was $25.4 billion.

The construction of the Panama Canal is the only project which rivaled the size of the Apollo space program in nonmilitary technological endeavors undertaken by the United States.

The Manhattan project was the only endeavor comparable in a wartime setting. The size of the Apollo space program was enormous and had one overall goal, a manned lunar landing.

President Kennedy delivered his famous Moon Speech at Rice University in Houston, Texas on 12 September 1962. In this unforgettable oration our Nation's leader committed America to being the first country to land a man on the moon and return him safely to earth.

There always have been and always will be doubters and naysayers who criticize the goals and ideas of leaders who are blessed with vision.

The 30 April 1964 addition of New Scientist Magazine reported, *"the odds now are that the United States will not be able to honor the 1970 manned lunar - landing date set by Mr. Kennedy".*

There is always a certain level of arrogance associated with doubt and that statement is undeniable proof.

The jeers of the unbelievers were silenced on 20 July 1969 when Apollo Eleven, manned by Neil A. Armstrong, Edwin E. "Buzz" Aldrin and Michal Collins landed on the moon's surface.

The words of Neil Armstrong will live on in history forever. *"That's one small step for a man and one giant leap for all mankind."*

The United States continued the Apollo Program and made nine more successful manned lunar landings.

The American Shuttle Program took the place of the capsule era. NASA was more impressed with the shuttle's ability to take off vertically and glide to an unpowered airplane-like landing.

NASA launched its first shuttle on 12 April 1981 and since that time there have been 130 + shuttle missions.

The majority have been successful while several have been fatal. Seventy-three seconds after it launched on 28 January 1986 the Space Shuttle Challenger exploded, killing all seven crew members on board.

NASA declared the cause of the fatality to be a leak in the joints of one of the two Solid Rocket Boosters attached to the Challenger Orbiters. The leak caused the main liquid fuel tank to explode.

Tragedy also occurred on 1 February 2003 when the Space Shuttle Columbia exploded on re-entry into the earth's atmosphere.

The cause of this accident was determined to be damage sustained during launch when a piece of foam insulation the size of a small briefcase broke off the space shuttle external tank (the main propellant tank) under the aerodynamics of launch.

The debris struck the leading edge of the left wing damaging the Shuttle's Thermal Protection System. This system is what protects the shuttle from heat generated with the atmosphere during re-entry.

NASA has had numerous accomplishments since 1958 and they are certainly to be praised for their perseverance in the face of adversity.

According to Wikipedia, "SETI stands for, Search for Extra-terrestrial Intelligence, a collective name for a number of activities people undertake to search for intelligent extra-terrestrial life".

NASA performed SETI projects until 1992 when funding for their program was cancelled. Public outrage was at a high enough level to persuade Congress to reopen the Roswell files for public inspection. (No doubt a lame peace offering)

There is no way to pinpoint an exact beginning for SETI because of what the four letters stand for. Individuals have been looking to the skies in search of Extra-Terrestrial neighbors for centuries.

According to, *The Search for Extraterrestrial Intelligence: a Short History*, by: Amir Alexander, Modern SETI does have a clear beginning.

In 1958 Phillip Morrison and Giuseppe Cocconi were physicists at Cornell University. Cocconi asked Morrison if he thought that gamma rays were the very medium of communication between the stars, Morrison agreed that gamma rays would work, but suggested that the entire electromagnetic spectrum should be considered for possibilities.

The result of this conversation was a short two page article entitled *Searching for Interstellar Communications*. This article was published in the 19 September 1959 edition of Nature Magazine and is known as SETI'S founding document.

The SETI Institute in Mountain View, California was founded in 1980 and continues to study Extra-Terrestrial Intelligence with the assistance of private contributions.

America's interest with this subject peaked on the morning of 08 July 1947 with news reports of a crashed flying disk near the Air Force base at Roswell, New Mexico.

The U.S. Military immediately called a press conference in which personnel stated that nothing more than a weather balloon had crashed and even presented for inspection the remnants of a weather balloon.

I have never been much of a conspiracy theorist, however if a missile hits a government facility and they want you to believe that it was an airplane all they have to do is call a press conference and show you the remnants of a crashed airplane. I am not calling the American government a liar; I am only indicating those in control at that time to be deceptive.

There were other discoveries to follow and I have included the ones I was able to find.

Aztec, New Mexico – 11 March 1948 – U.S. Military discovered a crashed flying disk containing 16 humanoid bodies ranging in height from 36 to 42 inches. All 16 were deceased.

Albuquerque, New Mexico – 10 September 1950 – Crashed flying disk, 3 bodies recovered.

Carlsbad, New Mexico – 18 July 1957 – Craft reported to have been in excellent condition, 4 bodies recovered.

Holloman AFB, New Mexico – 12 June 1962 – Crashed disk, 2 bodies recovered.

Chili, New Mexico – U.S. Air Force recovered a sixty foot wide metallic object. The object was transferred to Kirtland AFB.

I will begin by asserting without apology that I believe in the existence of Intelligent Extra-Terrestrial Life. Whether or not that life is human and can communicate with our Creator I do not know and will not even provide an assumption.

The one thing I notice in almost every crash story is that the occupants of the craft are deceased. I have often wondered, as I'm sure you have also, What if just one crash produced a survivor with which we could converse and exchange information?

I am particularly interested in the incidents where the craft is in good shape but the occupants are deceased. It leads one to believe that perhaps there is some chemical in their atmosphere that is not found in ours and they need that chemical for survival. I am sure that perhaps there are chemicals in our atmosphere which may cause their demise.

I am sure that most Americans have observed the pictures and videos made in the days following the Roswell incident. The photos of those small bodies lying there on an autopsy table being cut open and studied left me wanting to say of the government *how dare they,* however; I realize that it was a necessary part of their duties to come to a conclusion as to what exactly these individuals were.

The most intriguing argument has been whether or not they were human. I have mixed emotions regarding the matter and cannot say for certain if they were human or just humanoid.

In the event they were human they are souls and like the

rest of us must one day stand before Almighty God and give an account for their behavior while in the bodies.

In the event they were only humanoid and more like monkeys the question would be who manufactured the flying saucer and taught them how to operate it?

In order to avoid being referred to as a scare monger I will state my firm belief that the human race is the apple of God's eye. I know with a certainty that our Creator will not allow us to be overtaken by an alien race.

There is a fact that many in the field of UFO studies do not like to discuss. We know for a fact that Germany was manufacturing flying saucers during World War Two.

I discovered during my research that Adolf Hitler began to suffer extreme loss as a result of the combined forces of the U.S. and England. These losses so infuriated him that he gave orders to his top scientists to construct a super weapon capable of moving quickly without detection. The results were circular metallic discs which could perform in just that fashion.

There were eyewitness reports of a flying saucer marked with the German Military's Iron Cross over the Thames River in 1944.

Germany was also rumored to be experimenting with human cloning as well and some have gone as far as to say that the Roswell bodies and others were the victims of imperfect human cloning.

I personally do not accept this theory because in the event the bodies were that small and underdeveloped therefore the brain would likewise be too small and underdeveloped to operate a piece of machinery as complex as a flying saucer.

I will for the sake of entertaining the doubters admit that there was found within the Roswell wreckage a computerized chip like nothing seen before which could have been used to operate the craft from a distance.

There are speculations that the American Government

has been harboring the remnants of crashed flying saucers and alien bodies at Wright-Patterson Air Force Base in Ohio.

The government denies these claims even though the rumors are consistent among the many that circulate them.

I was disturbed at the fact former U.S. President Bill Clinton during an interview on foreign soil after leaving office declared Roswell to have been a hoax. The former

American leader proceeded to say that another crash site was given that identity because America was conducting experiments that we didn't want anyone to know about.

I am certain without question that the skeptics were overjoyed to hear such a spill from a former President who had access to every single document pertaining to one of the most important occurrences in the history of our great nation.

The best way to make an outright lie believable is to have a high ranking official tell it over public media airwaves.

I am aware that the files concerning the Roswell incident are top secret and have been kept from the public eye for years. In the event the Roswell incident is something top secret and Congress cannot allow the complete release of all official documents for a former President to make the statement that it was all a hoax gives the wrong message.

In the event it was all a hoax then there would be no reason to keep the documents closed any longer and we as Americans deserve an answer as to why our government performed this hoax and what were their reasons.

I also heard a rumor that secret societies fabricated the flying saucer phenomenon and that what is referred to as the illuminati have been planning to control the world by creating public fear through the concept that we will be attacked by an Extra-Terrestrial race.

This has always been an interesting story and has some degree of creditability however I am not convinced.

I realize that my words are harsh, however; the outright

denial of the possibility of Intelligent Extra-Terrestrial existence when we have undeniable proof is also harsh.

In the event we were able to make contact, America could benefit technologically from interaction with other worldly beings. Who is to say that Germany did not acquire their ability to manufacture flying saucers from an Extra-Terrestrial source?

I realize the anger everyone would have toward Extra-Terrestrial Intelligence in the event it was proven that they assisted Germany during World War Two.

The most reasonable assertion is that Hitler convinced them they would be doing the right thing by helping with ethnic cleansing and the creation of a perfect race. The fact is he convinced an entire nation and its military as he ascended to the Chancellorship of Germany in 1939.

I am convinced that to deny the existence of life anywhere but earth when we could benefit from interaction is like refusing to buy earthquake insurance for your home when it is built right on a known fault line.

American society is quite different today than it was in 1947, especially in the area of tolerance. I am certain that if Germany made their way onto American soil with this type of equipment and human clones no more than two years after the end of World War Two we would have launched right back into conflict.

The United States seized much of Germany's top secret technology once the war ended. Many believe that Roswell and other sightings around that time can be accredited to the American Military trying out their newly discovered weaponry.

This explanation has become a cushion of comfort and in many cases a weapon for those who do not believe in the existence of intelligent life anywhere other than earth.

The fact that Germany was manufacturing flying saucers does provide a certain amount of questions which can and have been shot at the Roswell incident; however it fails to address all previous sightings, some as far back as the tenth and twelfth centuries.

I was able to find several pre-1947 reports and I will share two, the first of which occurred in the year 776 A.D. in France during the Saxon siege on Sigiburg Castle.

The Saxons surrounded the French and as both parties began to do battle there appeared over the Church a group of discs described as flaming shields.

The Saxons interpreted this to mean divine intervention on behalf of the French and retreated.

The second pre-1947 sighting is accredited to the great explorer Christopher Columbus who kept journals of his travels.

Columbus recorded in his journals that he had at times observed lights in the night sky which were brighter than any he had ever witnessed before. Observation however was not

The only report as he described how the lights descended with great speed, ascending into the water and reemerging before returning to the sky.

Those who doubt will always seek an explanation and shooting stars is the cushion of comfort on which they rest. I hate to cause a disturbance however shooting stars burn out before they hit the earth and they certainly do not bounce off of the ocean floor.

I have heard and agree that the laws of physics place limits on space travel by physical beings that rely on oxygen and other elements that are found on earth. The argument with which I disagree is that no matter how much technological advancement we are able to manufacture we cannot overcome these limits.

There are numerous obstacles to travelling through space at slow speed. There are meteors and asteroids which are as large as some American cities and are travelling at speeds which make them invisible to the naked eye.

I can see maneuvering around something stationary but when both objects are moving it certainly makes avoiding a collision more difficult. The negative argument to space travel concerning this scenario is that a craft travelling at the speed of light would be unable to maneuver around and through these objects.

The answer I provide is one of such simplicity that it falls under the term common sense. In the event an intelligent race has the ability to travel at the speed of light they obviously have some sort of global positioning system that could direct them through space.

I have also been confronted with the fact that even travelling at the speed of light a trip from earths nearest star which is twenty five trillion miles away would take a number of years and food supply would run short.

There are numerous answers to this scenario but the one that makes the most sense to me is that an intelligent race from another galaxy may not require the same amount of nourishment that we on earth require.

I am also aware that the faster a craft travels the more radiation it is exposed to. Radiation causes erosion to metal and other material and would eventually bring about mechanical failure.

I will answer this by referring back to the 1947 incident at Roswell, New Mexico in which those investigating the crash plainly stated that the recovered material was not anything that was manufactured on our planet, therefore they may have better material.

Those who doubt the existence of Intelligent Extra-Terrestrial life do not like to admit the fact that there is physical material yet to be discovered and manufactured.

The human race is the most intelligent and the apple of God's eye, however; we must realize that our Creator is more intelligent than we are and I am certain that he did not reveal everything to us in the Bible.

Despite the fact that the Bible is the full and complete word of Almighty God it deals with his relationship to earth. When we declare that we are the highest of *all* creation I feel that we limit God's creative freedom and insinuate that we own God when in fact he owns us.

Despite the numerous discoveries and technological advancements that have been developed as a result of Space Exploration and Extra-Terrestrial studies there are numerous opponents to these projects.

These opponents fall in three categories; Scientific, Legal and Religious. They make their arguments based on their own experiments, past legal action concerning similar scenarios and theirs and others interpretation of the scriptures.

Scientific

According to one web site, "Science is the concerted human effort to understand, or to understand better, the history of the natural world and how the natural world works, with observable physical evidence as the basis of that understanding. It is done through observation of natural phenomena, and/or through experimentation that tries to simulate natural process under controlled conditions."

I assume with a definition like that it would be nearly impossible for anyone in the field of science to oppose the study of the universe and the possibility of other intelligent life forms.

There are several scientific theories pertaining to Extra-Terrestrial life and not all involve flying saucers. Some of the theories are biochemical, evolutionary and morphological.

The biochemical requirements for life on earth are carbon, hydrogen, nitrogen, oxygen, phosphorus and sulfur (CHNOPS). There are also smaller amounts of numerous other elements needed in order to sustain life.

Life requires water as the solvent in which biochemical reactions take place. Carbon in certain amounts along with water and the other life forming elements may enable the formation of living organisms on other planets with a chemical make up and average temperature similar to earth.

Evolutionary life is basically what I just described, something evolving out of a mixture of chemicals.

I do not doubt the scientific ability to mix multiple chemicals and make one product because almost everything on a store shelf is a combination of chemicals.

I do not believe that the human race and animal kingdom evolved because I accept the Biblical account of creation however the possibility of life forming through chemical evolution does not strain my faith.

The morphological viewpoint is mainly associated with science fiction movies and pertains to physical features such as flight, sight, photosynthesis, and limbs, all of which are thought to have evolved several times here on earth. In the event these characteristics did evolve it is only logical that they would not exhibit difficulty doing so again.

The belief that intelligent alien life forms without the benefit of language may communicate through hand signals the same way hearing impaired humans do is one theory pertaining to morphology.

NASA has been doing research into the possibility of non human life on planets such as Mars and examining meteors which have fallen to earth. The belief is that there may be bacteria like life and this belief has basis.

The ALH84001 meteorite discovered in Antarctica and believed to have been formed from rock ejected from Mars contains what some scientists believe to be fossilized bacteria. In the event this is true there was and could possibly still be life on the red planet.

Scientists have also discovered methane in the atmosphere

of Mars and are currently conducting tests to discern its biological or abiotic origin.

In 2008 laboratory tests aboard NASA's Phoenix Mars Lander had identified water in a soil sample. There were further tests which concluded that liquid water could have been flowing on the red planet within the last ten years.

In February 2005 two NASA scientists, Carol Stoker and Larry Lemke stated that they had evidence of present life on Mars. The claims were based on methane signatures found in Mars atmosphere resembling the methane production of some forms of primitive life on earth. NASA officials soon denied the scientists claims and Stoker herself backed away from her initial assertions.

Europa, one of Jupiter's moons has a possible liquid water layer under its surface which may contain life.

NASA is also conducting indirect searches for Extra-Terrestrial life by seeking funding for what is referred to as a planet finder. According to my research as of 2010 NASA still had not received any funding for the project.

There are extrasolar planets out there just waiting to be discovered. One that has already been discovered is Gliese 581 c. The fact that there are planets we did not know about means that there are planets we have yet to check for life.

SETI is constantly conducting astronomical searches for radio activity which would confirm the presence of intelligent life.

The last real signal that SETI detected was what is referred to as the WOW signal. The WOW signal was detected on 15 August 1977 by Dr. Jerry R. Ehman while working on a SETI project at the Big Ear radio telescope of the Ohio State University.

The signal lasted a total of 72 seconds and registered on the charts as 6EQUJ5. There were multiple numbers that appeared however any number over 3 was unusual and the only letters that appeared were E,Q,U and J.

There have been multiple searches performed over the years in hopes that the signal would reappear but there has been no luck.

There are as many theories as stars in the sky as to what the signal could have been. Some scientists' say that the signal was from earth and bounced off of something NASA had in flight while others are convinced that it originated in space.

There is no way to deny the possibility of life somewhere other than earth. That which was once considered science fiction is now science fact.

H.G. Wells done a great job in the early years with his *War of the Worlds* story that scared the daylights out of so many when the radio announcers failed to identify the broadcast as a radio play as opposed to real news reports.

I believe that Americans are now smart enough to discern the difference between science fiction and science fact. Whether the critics like it or not there more than likely is life somewhere other than this one planet we live on.

Legal

Those in the legal field generally agree with Space Exploration and Extra-Terrestrial research due to the revenue generated via representation of the insurance companies and families following the sometimes and unfortunate tragedies associated with these projects.

There is however a question of legality concerning Extra-Terrestrial visitation to earth. I am not sure what the policy is with any government including the United States because every time in the past that this situation has occurred the powers that be have masterfully and skillfully covered up every inch of the truth by using every possible excuse from weather balloons to crashed aircraft.

I am of the opinion that in the event an Extra-Terrestrial

race did dock on earth they should be required to remain on a Military instillation for the entire time they are here.

There is a rumor that in 1954 President Dwight D. Eisenhower met with Extra-Terrestrials at an Air Force base in California. I have read statements given by those who were present during the meeting and how they felt regarding the matter.

I am sure that we would not allow the Chinese government to roam the streets and country side in tanks and jeeps with their weapons in tow so therefore why should we permit an other worldly race to do the same thing and in the process scare the day lights out of everyone and their children.

I will say for the most part that the most memorable and important occurrence in the history of Extra Terrestrial research was the Roswell incident. It has kept America captivated since 1947 and will no doubt continue to attract attention for years to come.

There is only one political action committee to represent those in the field of ufology. That committee is X-PPAC in Bethesda, Maryland. X-PPAC stands for Extra-Terrestrial Phenomenon Political Action Committee.

The founder and director of X-PPAC is Steven Bassett who since the last of 2008 has been heading up the Million Fax on Washington.

The goal of this project is to have one million people fax the White House demanding that the Roswell files be opened to the general public and end the truth embargo that has hindered full disclosure since 1947.

I support the efforts of Mr. Bassett and those who work for and with him. I wish them the best of luck and hope that eventually they are successful in their goals.

Religious

I am a Born-Again Christian myself and I accept the Holy Bible to be the full and complete word of Almighty God. I do interpret some scripture different than most religious leaders and make no apologies for the fact. I do however wish to make it clear that it is simply a difference in interpretation and not me twisting the scriptures in order to enhance my own personal philosophy.

I feel that prior to expressing my own theology it is important to provide you with several quotes that have come from those who have been schooled in the area of religion.

Lutheran apologist Ted Peters asserts that questions raised by the possibility of extra-terrestrial life are by no means new to Christian theology and by no means pose a threat to Christian dogma as asserted by other authors.

Corrado Balducci, the Catholic Vatican theologian often discussed the question of Extra-Terrestrial existence in Italian popular media. In 2001 he published a statement entitled *UFOs and Extra-Terrestrials – A Problem for the Church?*

Jose Gabriel Funes, head of the Vatican Observatory said "Just as there is a multiplicity of creatures on Earth, there can be other beings, even intelligent, created by God."

C.S. Lewis, the Christian writer, in an article in the Christian Herald contemplated the possibility of the Son of God incarnating in other, Extra-Terrestrial worlds, or else that God would devise an entirely distinct plan of salvation for Extra-Terrestrial communities from the one applicable to humans.

I personally do not subscribe to that line of thinking because I accept the one death, one burial and one resurrection of Christ Jesus as being sufficient to save human souls regardless of where they may have been conceived and born and where they may live.

There are several passages of scripture that religious leaders have used over the years in order to make their argument against man exploring space. I will provide you with these verses and then I will explain what they mean to both sides.

There are two scriptures I want you to keep in mind as we explore other areas in God's word. The first is.

> "Study to shew thyself approved unto God,
> a workman that needeth not to be ashamed,
> rightly dividing the word of truth".
> 2 Timothy 2:15
> KJV 1611

This is the most important verse in the entire Bible when you are searching the scriptures for answers to tough questions. I want to make it clear that I will not declare a verse to mean something it does not mean just to suit my own opinion.

The second verse I want you to keep in mind is.

> "Neither give heed to fables and endless
> genealogies, which minister questions, rather
> than godly edifying which is in faith: *so do*".
> 1 Timothy 1:4
> KJV 1611

I realize that there is a certain amount of hesitation in the Christian community when it comes to discussion of Space Exploration and Extra-Terrestrial research. There are a lot of questions surrounding whether or not we are alone in the universe and most Christians would rather just say the Bible doesn't mention it so why discuss it.

I believe that we need to discuss these issues because the world is discussing them. There are scientists and physicists who are very influential and the influence they carry many times is not on the side of Christianity. I will not minister questions I will answer them.

James Grey

The world isn't speaking up for us and they consider us to be antiquated because we will not get with it as the old saying goes.

I am convinced that almost everything taught is a rewording and misrepresentation of the scriptures and if possible I want to expose the truth. I am certain that no scientist will argue with that statement because true science is a search for the truth.

With that said lets begin.

"And God made two great lights; the greater
light to rule the day, and the lesser light to
rule the night: *he made* the stars also".
Genesis 1:16
KJV 1611

"And God blessed them, and God said unto them,
Be fruitful and multiply, and replenish the earth,
and subdue it: and have dominion over the fish of
the sea, and over the fowl of the air, and over every
living thing that moveth upon the earth".
Genesis 1:28
KJV 1611

"And they said, Go to, let us build us a city
and a tower, whose top *may reach* unto heaven;
and let us make us a name, lest we be scattered
abroad Upon the face of the whole earth".
Genesis 11:4
KJV 1611

"And lest thou lift up thine eyes unto heaven, and when
thou seest the sun, and the moon, and the stars, *even*
all the host of heaven, shouldest be driven to worship
them, and serve them, which the Lord thy God hath
divided unto all nations under the whole heaven".
Deuteronomy 4:19
KJV 1611

"The heaven, even the heavens, are the Lord's: but
the earth hath he given to the children of men".
Psalm 115:16
KJV 1611

Every one of these scriptures is the inspired word of
Almighty God. Moses wrote the first four, the fifth is in the
book of Job and the sixth is found in the book of Psalms.

I listed them in the order they fall in the Bible however I
may not explain them in that particular order.

Genesis 1:16 says that God made two great lights and it
does not take a great mind to figure out that those two great
lights are the sun and the moon. There is an argument that
because these bodies were given to light the earth that man
should not attempt to access them.

Genesis 1:28 says that God told man to be fruitful and
replenish he earth. Man was given dominion over the earth
and all of its non human inhabitants. The argument against
Space Exploration is that man was given dominion over the
earth and therefore he should remain confined to it.

I want to take a look at Deuteronomy 4:19 as it flows
right along with the two verses we have already studied. The
sun, moon and stars have been divided among all nations so
therefore the argument has been made that it did not matter
who set foot on an astral body first given that it did not belong
to anyone.

I agree that the astral bodies belong only to the Creator
and no nation or human being has the right or the might to
claim ownership. I do not however agree with the statement
that it did not matter who won the race to the moon because
nations will war against nations.

America was in the 1960s a far better nation than the
Soviet Union which was still under heavy Communist rule and
treated its people far less than respectable.

America had a point to make and I am comfortable that we made that point. I am also comfortable that the fact an American flag was the first to be planted in the moon's soil also sets a standard for space exploration.

The late Walter Lang argued in favor of space exploration using Genesis 1:16 as his basis *"Since the astral bodies were made for the earth, and since man is to subdue the earth, man is justified in extending his reach to the planets and the stars."*

I feel that this particular argument covers these three verses. God gave man dominion over the earth and all of its non human inhabitants. God gave us the astral bodies to light the earth and he gave mankind a brain with which the Creator knew we would eventually venture toward the heavens once we grew bored down here.

Psalm 115:16 says that the heavens belong to God but the earth he gave to the children of men.

Genesis 11:4 seems to be most popular basis for religious argument against Space Exploration as it shows God's wrath on those who conceived in their hearts that they would build a tower which would reach all the way into heaven.

There are those who feel that modern Space Exploration falls under the same wrong doing and arrogance as the tower of Babel of which Genesis 11:4 speaks.

There is no way that I can agree with that philosophy because America's intent is not by any means the same as those who wanted to ascend all the way into heaven.

There are three heavens, the first heaven we see with our eyes, Genesis 1:8, the second heaven we can see only with a telescope, Genesis 15:5 and the third heaven which is the abode of God and no man will see without having been born again, 2 Corinthians 12:2.

I feel that in the event modern man's intentions were the same as the Babylonians then God would have caused the man who invented the telescope to speak an unknown language.

The scriptures I have addressed up to now are the ones

uscd to argue against Space Exploration, the scriptures used to argue against the existence of Extra-Terrestrial intelligence are different and I chose to address them separately.

> "And God said, Let the earth bring forth the living creature after his kind, cattle, and creeping thing, and beast of the earth after his kind: and it was so".
> Genesis 1:24
> KJV 1611

> "And he said unto them, I beheld Satan as lightning fall from heaven".
> Luke 10:18
> KJV 1611

> "And the Lord said unto Satan, Whence comest thou? Then Satan answered the Lord, and said, From going to and fro in the earth, and walking up and down in it".
> Job 1:7
> KJV 1611

I stated before and I will state again that I accept the Bible to be the inspired word of Almighty God and if the Bible says it then I believe it.

Genesis 1:24 clearly states that everything upon the earth came from the earth.

I have heard the theory that the human race is descended of an extra-terrestrial race often referred to as the Anunnaki. I do not accept this due to the following scriptures.

> "So God created man in his own image, in the image of God created he him; male and female created he them".
> Genesis 1:27
> KJV 1611

"And the Lord God formed man of the dust of
the ground, and breathed into his nostrils the
breath of life; and man became a living soul".
Genesis 2:7
KJV 1611

"And the Lord God caused a deep sleep to fall upon
Adam, and he slept: and he took one of his ribs,
and closed up the flesh instead thereof; And the rib
which the Lord God had taken from man, made
he a woman, and brought her unto the man".
Genesis 2:21-22
KJV 1611

Luke 10:18 is a statement made by Christ Jesus himself concerning the fall of Lucifer. Lucifer was God's most beautiful angel and his name means *bringer of light.*

The chief reason for his creation was to bring honor and glory to Almighty God; however he rebelled and was cast out of heaven. One third of the angel population followed him to earth and that is where they remain in spirit form to this very day.

There are stories that have been passed down since ancient times concerning gods who came down from heaven and mated with earth women. Their descendents are referred to as the Anunnaka.

I am sure that everyone is familiar with the practice of taking the truth and rewording it so that it makes an entirely different story. The story of the Anunnaki is just that, a rewording of the truth.

The truth is there were powerful beings that came down from heaven but they did not necessarily make the trip willingly and have ever since been waging war with Almighty God.

The theory of gods from the heavens mating with earth women may have some Biblical backing; however there is some difference in interpretation concerning the following scripture.

"And it came to pass, when men began to multiply on the face of the earth, and daughters were born unto them, That the sons of God saw the daughters of men that they *were* fair; and they took them wives of all which they chose".
Genesis 6:1-2
KJV 1611

This scripture has often been interpreted to mean that the fallen angels married earth women and produced children by them. I have no reason to dispute this particular interpretation however it would not be appropriate if I did not provide you with the other interpretation.

Adam and Eve, the first couple had two sons, Cain and Abel. Genesis Chapter 4 tells how Cain killed his brother and God banished him to the land of Nod on the East of Eden. There Cain knew his wife and they had children.

God allowed Adam and Eve to produce another son and they called his name Seth. The alternate interpretation of Genesis 6:1-2 is that the sons of God were the descendents of Seth while the daughters of men were the descendents of Cain.

I am partial to the first interpretation because it says the sons of God married the daughters of men. Angels have always been referred to as being male. What would have been the reference in the event a male descendent of Cain married a female descendent of Seth? Would the Bible have said *a son of man married a daughter of God?*

The second interpretation insinuates that all descendents of Seth were male and all descendents of Cain were female.

I believe this scripture to be the origin for the theory of humans descending of an Extra-Terrestrial race. I am confident that I have provided you with enough information that you can see the misunderstanding in the interpretation.

Job 1:7 says that Satan told God how he was going to and fro in the earth and walking up and down in it. The argument has been made that in the event there is human life anywhere but earth why is Satan not seeking to harvest those souls as well?

I stated earlier that there is always the possibility that Extra-Terrestrial life is nonhuman and does not have the ability to communicate with the Creator.

I feel that I have successfully proven by interpretation that none of these scriptures speak negatively toward Space Exploration or Extra-Terrestrial research.

There are certain scriptures that have been used to insinuate that Extra-Terrestrial intelligence visited the writers of the Bible however; I am not convinced that that is what they mean.

Ezekiel chapter 1 describes visions experienced by the writer. The visions were that of beings with four faces and four wings coming out of a whirlwind. Ezekiel described wheels within wheels as the creatures moved with the quickness of a flash of lightning. This description is what has led many to conclude that the vision was simply an encounter with a space ship.

The remainder of the book of Ezekiel clears up the whole matter as we read the words spoken from the whirlwind by Almighty God when he told Ezekiel to go minister to the land of Israel and the results of Ezekiel's obedience.

There is no way to deny the fact that there is no reference to Extra-Terrestrial intelligence in the scriptures.

In the event it is out there I wish the Creator would have mentioned it in his word however he is God and what he does he does and what he does not he does not, its just that simple.

I have encountered questions regarding whether or not the

Bible says anything at all about the modern UFO phenomenon such as the Roswell incident and reported abductions.

I have heard that the following scripture references the very subject.

"Then I turned, and lifted up mine eyes, and looked, and behold a flying roll. And he said unto me, What seest thou? And I answered, I see a flying roll; the length thereof is twenty cubits, and the breadth thereof ten cubits".
Zechariah 5:1-2
KJV 1611

This particular scripture on first reading seems to provide a very good description of a flying saucer, however; if you read on you will find that it has nothing to do with modern sightings.

"Then he said to me, This is the curse that goeth forth over the face of the whole earth: for every one that stealeth shall be cut off as on this side according to it; and every one that sweareth shall be cut off as on that side according to it".
Zechariah 5:3
KJV 1611

In the event this scripture is referencing modern encounters the only assumption I can make is that everyone who sees a UFO is a thief and one who swears.

"Then the angel that talked with me went forth, and said unto me, Lift up now thine eyes, and see what is this that goeth forth. And I said, What is it? And he said, This is an ephah that goeth forth. He said moreover, This is their resemblance through all the earth. And behold, there was lifted up a talent of lead: and this is a woman that sitteth in the midst of the ephah. And he said, This is wickedness. And he cast it into the midst of the ephah; and he cast the weight of lead upon the mouth thereof. Then lifted I up mine eyes, and looked, and, behold, there came out two women, and the wind was in their wings; for they had wings like the wings of a stork: and they lifted up the ephah between the earth and the heaven. Then said I to the angel that talked with me, Whither do these bear the ephah? And he said unto me, To build it an house in the land of Shinar: and it shall be established, and set there upon her own base".

Zechariah 5:5-11

KJV 1611

I have heard it interpreted that this scripture is talking about the fallen angels. Talent of lead, in the Bible's original languages, means metallic disk.

I can see where that would lead one to the flying saucer interpretation and I am in no way criticizing those who interpret this scripture in that way. I see so many things that fit the description of a metallic disk, *such as hubcaps on a vehicle,* that I'm sure every metallic disc is not demonic.

I looked up the definition of ephah and discovered that it is a basket. I have viewed many pictures of UFOs and flying saucers and have yet to see anything that even remotely resembles a basket being carried by two women with wings like a stork.

I did some research into Zechariah Chapter 5 and discovered that it is actually talking about how God plans to deal with the nation of Israel as pertains to their sin against him. I am not sure where the modern UFO interpretation was obtained.

I have read the stories of those who were abducted and in many cases there may very well have been demonic activity.

The following scripture gives the best definition of demons I have found.

"For we wrestle not against flesh and blood, but
against principalities, against powers, against
the rulers of the darkness of this world, against
spiritual wickedness in high *places*".
Ephesians 6:12
KJV 1611

The point I am attempting to make here is that demons
are not physical, they are spiritual, and they are not able to be
physically active unless they enter some living creature.

The fact is they have been in the spiritual form ever since
their physical bodies were drowned in the flood.

I have heard some say that the Roswell bodies and others
were fallen angels and that fallen angels were different than
demons.

I am not able to accept this theory due to the Roswell
bodies being physical and the existence of, *whether they will
admit it or not*, autopsy reports. There never has and never will
be an autopsy performed on a spirit.

The theory has always been that demons could only
operate through human beings and not animals. This theory
comes from the fact that only humans have a soul and the
human soul is the craving of Satan and his fallen.

I am certain that for the most part this is correct; however
I recall the Biblical account in Matthew 8:28-32 of the demons
leaving the man and entering the swine.

The demons guided the pigs down the hill and into the
water where they drowned. I take from this scripture that
demons can operate through the animal kingdom, if for
nothing else than to kill off someone's live stock and cause
them loss.

I am certain that there are many more verses which
indicate demonic activity in the modern UFO phenomenon
and I would love to address them as well. My overall goal for
this work however is not to explain the entire Bible but rather

to address the overall situation and the spiritual philosophies associated with it.

I have been asked numerous times, In the event there is intelligent human life somewhere besides earth where did they come from and who is their Savior?

I feel that right here is the best place to give my personal opinion as to where they came from.

In 2 Kings 2:11 we read that Elijah did not die because God took him up into Heaven and in Hebrews 11:5 we read how God done the same thing with Enoch.

I personally believe that God used the physical DNA of these two men to start new races in other galaxies. They and their offspring are subject to the same sin debt as we are due to their being descendents of Adam and Eve. This means that they must be saved in the same way those of us here on earth.

"For God so loved the world, that he gave his only begotten Son, that whosoever believeth in him should not perish, but have everlasting life".
John 3:16
KJV 1611

I am convinced that when Jesus Christ came to earth, where sin began, in the form of a man, with whom sin began and gave his life for the human soul, which was the only thing needing a Savior, that his one death, one burial and one resurrection covered the sin debt for all mankind regardless of where he is, whether that be here on earth or on the back side of some galaxy millions of light years from earth.

God will one day destroy the earth and everything in it with the exception of those human souls that have accepted his offer of salvation which is made through his Son, Christ Jesus; *in the following manner.*

"For by grace are ye saved through faith; and
not of yourselves: *it is* the gift of God: Not
of works, lest any man should boast".
Ephesians 2:8
KJV 1611

Who needs a Savior?

"For all have sinned and come short of the glory of God".
Romans 3:23
KJV 1611

Who can save us?

"Neither is there salvation in any other: for
there is none other name under heaven given
among men, whereby we must be saved".
Acts 4:12
KJV 1611

How are we saved?

"That if thou shalt confess with thy mouth the Lord
Jesus, and shalt believe in thine heart that God hath
raised him from the dead, thou shalt be saved".
Romans 10:9
KJV 1611

There are numerous religions in the world today but there
remains only one way to be saved and have an assured spot in
heaven.

The plan of salvation is as simple as ABC.

1 – ADMIT – That you are a sinner. Romans 3:23

2 – BELIEVE – That Jesus Christ is the only way of salvation. Acts 4:12

3 – CONFESS – Jesus Christ as Lord. Romans 10:9

I would not have accomplished my goal unless I provided you with what is commonly referred to as the sinner's prayer. In the event you would like to be saved, simply pray the following prayer.

> Heavenly Father, I admit that I am a sinner. I believe that you sent your only begotten son in order to prepare a way for me to be saved. I believe that he suffered and died and that you raised him from the dead. I confess with my mouth that Jesus Christ is the only name given under heaven among men whereby we must be saved. Lord Jesus, please forgive me of my sins, come into my heart and be my Savior. I make you the Lord of my life. In Jesus name I pray, Amen.

In the event you prayed this prayer and meant it in your heart you were just adopted into the family of Almighty God. You are now one of his children and a brother or sister to every other Christian there ever was, is and will be.

I realize that those who were already opposed to Space Exploration and Extra-Terrestrial studies will more than likely remain opposed. I did not set out to recruit the world to my way of thinking but to expound upon the love our creator has for us and to bring as many people to him as possible.

In the event you have become a Christian while reading this book I would like to hear from you. I cannot promise a response to everyone but just knowing it would make my day. I can be contacted at *BookOnUniversalAuthority@gmail.com*.

I have enjoyed providing you with a history of NASA and its projects. I have even provided you with the sour spills of its opponents and the sweetness of the moments the dreams were realized.

I am without apology in favor of Space Exploration and Extra-Terrestrial studies. I will not back up on this stand because there is nothing more important than knowing, or at least trying to know, what is out there.

I read a statement in response to a You Tube video on Space Exploration that after making a total of nine successful moon landings with a total of twelve men walking on the moon's surface the United States has for some reason remained close to earth in its shuttle missions.

I believe that America should make it a priority to return to the moon in 2019 as a fiftieth anniversary celebration of the first successful manned lunar-landing. I would also support naming the vehicle in honor of the men who made that first successful voyage.

PART 2

SCIENCE, PHYSICS AND
TIME TRAVEL

Science, Physics and Time Travel

*"If a man will begin with certainties, he shall
end in doubts; but if he will be content to begin
with doubts, he shall end in certainty".*
- Francis Bacon

Every human being is different and every human being has
God given talents and abilities that lie just waiting to be
discovered.

In this chapter I will present to you the stories and
accomplishments of several individuals who made a difference
in the every day lives of people everywhere. These individuals
all had and or have vision beyond anything the ordinary mind
can conceive.

In many cases they were considered to be insane by others
in their field as well as made fun of and ridiculed, right up to,
if not beyond their deaths. Today we look back and see what
those before us could not see.

I am confident that if we will open our eyes to the limitless
possibilities in science and physics we will celebrate the past
and encourage the future.

I assume that nearly every home in America has electricity
and a telephone. These luxuries were discovered and or invented
by scientists and physicists.

Electricity is a natural element which has been harnessed
and used in a productive manner as a result of laboratory
study.

The invention of the telephone was contested in a legal
battle between Alexander Graham Bell and Elisha Gray. Both

men applied for patents for their inventions on the same day, within hours of one another.

Alexander Graham Bell won due to the fact that he arrived at the patent office first and has since been known as the inventor of the telephone.

Alexander Bell was born on 3 March 1847 in Edinburgh, Scotland to Alexander Melville and Eliza Symonds Bell.

The son and grandson of authorities in elocution "the study of formal speaking in pronunciation, grammar, style and tone", Bell himself obtained an education and taught in the same subjects.

In 1858 Alexander Bell adopted the name Graham out of admiration for Alexander Graham who was a family friend.

In 1876 at the age of twenty-nine Bell invents his version of the telephone and performed the first successful test on 10 March of that same year.

Bell's research notebook contained the results of a conversation between himself and his assistant Thomas Watson who was in another room of the house at the time. *"Mr. Watson – come here – I want to see you"*.

This was no doubt the very first telephone call and words that deserve the same recognition and respect as those spoken when America landed on the moon.

In 1877 Alexander Graham Bell formed the Bell telephone company and settled into a life of financial security in which he was able to set his own schedule.

That same year Bell married Mabel Hubbard whose father Gardiner Hubbard had contributed financially to the invention of the telephone. Mabel was hearing impaired and was one of Bell's students at the school where he taught elocution and speech.

Amazingly Bell's overall ambition in life was not to make more money for himself but to contribute as much of his knowledge and ability as possible to the world's technological advancement.

Bell was awarded the Volta Prize, of ten thousand dollars in 1880; an award created by Napoleon Bonaparte to honor Italian Physicist Alessandro Volta who was accredited with inventing the battery, this award was given to someone for scientific achievement in electricity.

The prize was given to Bell for his invention of the telephone and he used the money for himself and two other scientific men to carry on experimental research.

The great scientist and inventor passed away on 2 August 1922 in Baddeck, Nova Scotia, Canada but had gone on to invent many useful items which have since been improved on and are still in use today.

I wish to expand on the life of inventor Elisha Gray who had requested a patent for his version of the telephone on the same day as Alexander Graham Bell.

Elisha Gray was an Engineer/Inventor who was born on 2 August 1835 in Barnesville, Ohio to a Quaker family and raised on a farm.

Gray attended Oberlin College and experimented with electrical devices, though he did not graduate he spent several years there teaching electricity and sciences and built lab equipment for their science departments. While at Oberlin in 1862 Elisha Gray met and married Delia Minerva Shepard.

In 1869 Gray and his partner Enos M. Barton founded the Gray Barton Company in Cleveland, Ohio to supply telegraph equipment to the great Western Union Telegraph Company.

In 1872 Western Union bought one third of the Gray Barton Company and it eventually became known as Graybar Electric.

Elisha Gray invented the telautograph in 1887. This machine was an early version of the modern fax machine. Gray received a patent for his invention in 1888.

According to Wikipedia, "the telautograph operated by transmitting electrical impulses which are recorded by potentiometers at the sending station to servomechanisms attached to a pen at the receiving station thus reproducing at the receiving station a drawing or signature made by the sender".

The Franklin Institute awarded Gray the Elliot Cresson Medal for the invention of the telautograph in 1897.

The Elliot Cresson Medal was created by its name sake in 1848 and was awarded for some discovery in the arts and sciences, the invention or improvement of some useful machine, some new process or combination of materials in manufacturing or for ingenuity, skill or perfection in workmanship.

Cresson was a life member of the Franklin Institute. The medal was first awarded in 1875 and last awarded in 1997.

There are other scientists and physicists who have contributed greatly to the comfortable lives we now live.

Allesandro Volta, for whom voltage is named, invented the electrochemical cell, more commonly known as the battery. What would some people do without their Walkmans?

Georg Simon Ohm discovered the direct proportionality between the potential differences (voltage) applied across a conductor and the resultant electric current which is now known as Ohm's law.

Thomas Edison invented the light bulb which no doubt brightened up our lives and cut down on America's vision problems by reducing eye strain due to reading by the dimness of a coal oil or kerosene lamp.

Nikola Tesla was the first to experiment with wireless energy transfer between towers. I read that he was dismissed as a mad scientist by the experts of his day and died nearly broke.

In the event we are allowed cell phones in heaven I think they should be named in his honor.

The most interesting and exciting experiment I have ever studied is what was referred to as the Philadelphia Experiment.

The Philadelphia Experiment was a study of Unified Field

Theory, an idea first introduced by the great physicist Albert Einstein.

Unified Field Theory aims to describe mathematically and physically the interrelated nature of the forces that comprise electromagnetic radiation and gravity.

The reason the U.S. Military was interested in its study is because it was supposed to enable the use of large electrical generators to bend light around an object making it completely invisible.

The tests were reported to have begun in the summer of 1943, the first of which was conducted on 22 July at the U.S. Naval shipyard in Philadelphia, Pennsylvania, with the USS Eldridge as the project's guinea pig.

The overseers administered an electromagnetic charge to the ships hull. The eyewitness reports state that this occurrence rendered the ship almost invisible while surrounded by a greenish fog. Some of those present complained of extreme nausea.

The real problem with the experiment occurred on board the ship when it was discovered that several sailors were embedded into the metal. The tests were halted at the request of the U.S. Navy.

Those involved received help for both medical and mental problems resulting from their participation in the experiment.

I imagine this experience was similar to a child on an outing with his Father who instructs his son on the proper usage of a firearm. The kick of the weapon knocks its inexperienced user to the ground. The experience, for a period of time, leaves the child fearful of guns.

The trembles and shakes apparently vanished and on 28 October 1943 the same experiment was conducted again.

The overseers once again administered an electromagnetic charge to the ships hull. The results this time were reported to be more intense as the USS Eldridge completely vanished in a flash of blue light and supposedly teleported to the U.S. Naval shipyard in Norfolk, Virginia.

Eyewitnesses in Norfolk stated that the USS Eldridge sat in full view of men on the SS Andrew Furuseth for some time before it vanished and reappeared in the U.S. Naval shipyard in Philadelphia. It was also reported that the Eldridge travelled back in time a total of ten seconds.

I discovered during the course of my study that many consider the entire experiment to be a hoax.

I personally disagree with the doubters and see the Philadelphia experiment not as science fiction but as science and physics, not as paranormal but rather perfectly normal.

I am convinced that if someone administers an electromagnetic charge to a metal table, and it vanishes, anyone standing on it would fall to the floor.

The moment the table reappears the person who fell and is standing in the center thereof would be entrapped within the table.

I do not believe that there would be a hole in the middle where the individual is standing because that part of the table has reappeared as well, they are now a part of the table and the table is a part of them.

In the event a second electromagnetic charge is administered, causing the table to vanish once again, the individual could be pulled free with no severances or lacerations as the molecular structure of the individual and the table would remain intact.

I cannot and will not even attempt to explain the teleportation, as that is neither my specialty nor intention by this work.

The one area of science and physics that intrigues me more than any is the concept of time travel.

According to Wikipedia, "Time Travel is the concept of moving between different points in time in a manner analogous to moving between different points in space, either sending objects (or in some cases just information) backwards in time to some moment before the present, or sending objects forward from the present to the future without the need to experience the intervening period (at least not at the normal rate)".

Time Travel has always been considered science fiction and was never studied in any seriousness until several years ago.

Dr. Ronald Mallett, Professor of Physics at the University of Connecticut, became fascinated with the concept of time travel following the death of his Father as the result of a heart attack.

I am certain that there is no one in America who has never heard of H.G. Well's *"The Time Machine"*. This great literary work was first published in 1895 and has always been in print by some publishing company.

Ronald Mallett writes in his memoir, *"Time Traveler, A Scientist's Personal Mission to make Time Travel a Reality"*, that his discovery of the comic book version of The Time Machine one year after his Father passed away was what brought him to an interest in science and physics.

The future scientist was intrigued by the notion of travelling back in time to warn his Father that he had a weak heart and needed to schedule a doctor's appointment.

This dream never left the young man as he grew into a teenager and then an adult. Mallett chose to join the U.S. Air force upon completion of high school and shipped out for training within two weeks after graduation.

Studying math through correspondence courses in his spare time, Mallett was preparing for a much higher education.

In 1973 he received his Ph.D. in physics from Pennsylvania State University and went on to become a professor of theoretical physics at the University of Connecticut.

I realize that there are many who feel themselves to be the sanest among the millions and potential world leaders.

These people have either chosen to live in mediocrity for

the sake of having more time to spend with their families and the betterment of all mankind or they find themselves stuck in normal every day occupations that they hate.

The reason or excuse for this occurrence is because someone else got the job they wanted as the result of having a friend or relative in a high enough position that their lack of qualifications were ignored.

These people will criticize and ridicule Dr. Mallett for holding onto his dream of time travel and say that he suffers from a mental disorder for which he should have but never did receive treatment.

I am convinced that those who criticize the success of others obviously have no vision of their own.

I have dreams, goals and aspirations that are deeply personal and the success of others does not and will not interfere with how quickly or slowly they are realized.

I can only imagine the pain and resentment felt by this young man upon being notified that his Father, his mentor and confidant would no longer be there for him. I myself felt that same sting at the age of six.

Anger is a form of emotion which can be used in either a positive or negative manner. Ronald Mallett or I either one could have joined a gang and gone around slashing tires, breaking windows, snatching purses, matching wits with Law Enforcement and comparing notes with the guys over a six pack of bud.

The fact that we both discovered famous men in history to look up to was the saving grace to which we owe our freedom, success and lives.

Dr.Mallett found Albert Einstein and I found John F. Kennedy. There is something that many people overlook and that is the fact of how children usually grow up to follow in the foot steps of those they idolize.

I realize that time travel for the most part has always

been considered science fiction and those who envision its possibilities considered disturbed.

There are always doubters who will look for the short in the wiring when a light comes on in someone's head, especially when that light doesn't seem to be aglow anywhere else.

I plan to expound on the subject of Time Travel in depth and answer the scientific, legal and religious questions associated with and surrounding the subject but first I would like to give a few examples of success regarding ideas rejected by the seasoned veterans of specific industries.

The first automobiles had stiff rubber tires with no air inside. There were numerous problems with this arrangement and one was the discomfort of a bumpy ride.

Harvey Firestone arrived at the conclusion that vehicle tires should have air inside, which would make the ride much smoother. Those to whom he presented his idea quickly stated their disagreement and advised him not to move forward with the plan.

I am grateful; as I'm sure you are too, that Harvey Firestone proceeded with his new invention. I imagine that not having to change a flat would be about the only positive note to stiff rubber tires.

In 1968 the Swiss held 65% of the worlds watch market with Japan having virtually no share. Ten years later in 1978 Japan held the major share and the Swiss had dropped to below 20%.

The quartz electronic watch was invented by the Swiss, however they rejected the invention stating hat it had no real relevance to the future of watch making and did not even bother taking out a patent to protect it.

Texas Instruments of the United States and Seiko of Japan took notice and the rest became history.

The seasoned veterans of both the tire and watch industry felt that everything of importance to their livelihood had already been invented.

They were now interested in maintaining a steady flow of the same old assembly line technology with which they were comfortable and did not welcome any confusing changes.

The Wright Brothers were sure that their invention of a flying machine would cooperate with the laws of physics despite the criticism and ridicule of others. These two men persevered in the face of adversity and today there are thousands of airplanes in the sky twenty-four seven.

I feel that it is important to show you just how many of the every day appliances we take for granted came close to not making the cut. Those in positions of power and influence were not always impressed with scientific break through and in many cases made their lack of satisfaction known.

Time Travel is one of those subjects that people either see as possible or they don't there is no other way to put it. I see it as possible and I am prepared to defend it with the results of my research, my words and word processor.

I will do the same with Time Travel that I did with Space Exploration and Extra-Terrestrial Research and answer the three unavoidable questions of Scientific, Legal and Religious. I made it clear in the introduction that unless they are addressed they will make their way into the conversations and/or debates on their own.

Scientific

The scientific questions surrounding the ability of a human being to physically travel between two points in time are probably the easiest to address. There has already been considerable research performed and the lines are completely drawn between both sides.

The most popular scientific equation that has been used in defense of the ability to travel in time is $E=mc2$.

According to Wikipedia, "Special Relativity (SR, also

known as Special Theory of Relativity or STR) is the physical theory of measurement in internal frames of reference, proposed in 1905 by Albert Einstein.

In Einstein's famous equation c is the speed of light in a vacuum. There are consequences to the theory and one is that it is impossible for any particle that has rest mass to be accelerated to the speed of light.

The theory of special relativity generalizes Galileo's principle of relativity – that all uniform motion is relative, and that there is no absolute and well-defined state of rest (no privileged reference frames) – from mechanics to all the laws of physics, including both the laws of mechanics and electrodynamics, whatever they may be".

The theory of special relativity allows for Time Travel into the future provided that the person and/or object are moving at the speed of light and since there is no absolute and well-defined state of rest I am certain that the door is open to possibility.

There are other scientific theories as to what might allow for Time Travel into both the past and the future.

Black holes are the product of a collapse of a massive star that has such an extreme gravitational force that it keeps light particles from leaving its surface, making the star practically invisible.

There is but one objective to a black hole and that is to pull you in. There is no way to reemerge from the same entrance given the force of its gravitational pull.

Roy Kerr, a mathematician from New Zealand, studied black holes. In the 1960s Kerr declared that in the event a black hole is rotating then a singularity forms in the shape of a ring.

According to Kerr's findings it would be possible to dive into such a space and through the ring, emerge in another place and time.

White holes are formed in the same way as black holes, the exception is, as opposed to pulling you in they spew you out.

There is a theory that black and white holes are connected by worm holes. If this theory is correct then you could be pulled into a black hole and shot through a worm hole at the speed of light into a white hole where you would emerge into a different place and time.

The problem with this form of Time Travel is finding a way home. The possibility of finding another black hole is pretty slim plus the probability that it would lead back to where you began is also highly unlikely.

Worm holes are created when gravity pushes matter together, creating singularities to close the worm hole. The worm hole would be able to stay open if a form of matter gives off a negative pressure which had antigravity associated with it.

According to Newton's third law of motion, any object that comes in contact with a force of equal and opposite force will be distributed. This means that the worm hole could not be closed off because the black hole is pushing, keeping the end connected to it open and the white hole is pulling the end connected to it therefore keeping it open as well.

Stephen Hawking, one of the greatest physicists of our times declared that Time Travel was not possible; however an Israeli researcher by the name of Amos Ori discovered a flaw in the argument put forth by Hawking.

Stephen Hawking once asked the question, *if Time Travel is possible then where are all of the time travelers from the future?*

The answer is invisibility. The United States government has been working for some time now on what is referred to as light bending. This is accomplished by wearing a garment made from special material around which light bends leaving the wearer invisible.

Dr. Ronald Mallett, the professor of physics at the University of Connecticut has been studying the subject of

Time Travel his entire career and has asserted his belief that Time Travel can be accomplished by bending light. Light which is energy can create gravity and in the process effect time.

Dr. Mallett built a model time machine in order to demonstrate his point. The model has four intersecting light beams and the region within that column of light would represent the region in which space is being twisted and eventually time would also get twisted by this column of light. The concept is that this would allow us to travel back into the past.

There is one thing however that must be kept in mind and that is the fact that you could only travel back to the point the time machine was turned on.

There is a theory in the scientific community that some Extra-Terrestrial race may already have the ability to travel in time.

This race may have invented and activated their device thousands of years ago and in the event we were able to communicate with them perhaps they would be willing to share their technology.

The laws of science, physics and mechanics are important and must never be forgotten or overlooked.

There is an area of science that is ignored by those who require irrefutable proof of everything, and that is pseudoscience.

According to Wikipedia, "Pseudoscience is a claim, belief or practice which is presented as scientific, but which does not adhere to a valid scientific method, lacks supporting evidence or plausibility, cannot be reliably tested or otherwise lacks scientific status.

Pseudoscience is often characterized by the use of vague, exaggerated or unprovable claims, an over-reliance on confirmation rather than rigorous attempts at refutation, a lack of openness to evaluation by other experts and a general absence of systematic processes to rationally develop theories.

Pseudoscientific thinking has been explained in terms of psychology and social psychology. The human proclivity for seeking confirmation rather than refutation (confirmation bias), the tendency to hold comforting beliefs, and the tendency to over generalize have been proposed as reasons for the common adherence to pseudoscientific thinking. Humans are prone to associations based on resemblances only and often prone to misattribution in cause-effect thinking".

I had to hold my breath as I read the article because with a description like that there is no limit to how many relevant scientific theories can be metaphorically tossed into this often misrepresented category.

I brought up the subject of pseudoscience because of the fact that Time Travel has been considered for years to fall into this definition. I feel that it needs to be rescued from a muddy swamp, cleaned up and presented in the clear waters of true science despite the fact that it has yet to be accomplished.

The subject of Time Travel paradoxes is of a certainty scientific. In the event you travel back in time and prevent the birth of Adolph Hitler you would more than likely stop or delay World War 2.

There were thousands of Americans killed in that unfortunate occurrence of world history. Their widows remarried and produced children by other men. If World War 2 were prevented from taking place then there are children who would never have been born.

There were women who used government death benefits to start businesses. The fact they did not lose their husband would prevent those businesses from becoming reality.

There is a theory to which I give validity and that is the theory of parallel universes. I have read during the course of my research that if you travel back in time you may find yourself in a parallel universe where everything seems to be the same when in fact it is not.

In the event you interfered with your parents becoming acquainted with one another then you would not be born. I have heard that if this were to actually take place then you would either immediately fade out or disappear on reentry to your original time line.

Hugh Everett III, a graduate of Princeton University came up with his many-worlds interpretation of quantum mechanics in 1957.

The many-worlds theory states that every decision we make breaks into two separate yet equal universes. If you are standing at the counter of a fast food restaurant and you must choose between a hamburger and a hotdog, the instant you make your choice there is another you in another universe that made the opposite choice.

The theory of parallel universes asserts that you would still exist because the time line on which you interfered with your parents first meeting is not the same one on which you live.

In the event you travel into the past and interfere with original occurrences you will not only create a paradox you will be left to live out your life in the past as a part of that paradox and history as well.

If something of this nature were to take place I am sure that the memory of every single human being in existence would be instantly changed and therefore any legal action against you would not be possible.

I do not believe that it would be appropriate to end this section without mentioning the one Time Travel story that apparently no one has been able to debunk and that is the story of John Titor.

In November of 2000 a man calling himself John Titor began posting on internet message boards that he was a Time Traveler from the year 2036. These posts continued until

March of 2001 at which time John indicated that he had to return to his original time line.

John stated that he was a member of the United States Military who had been sent back to 1975 to acquire an IBM 5100 computer which had certain abilities that were needed on his time line. John went on to say that he had stopped in 2000 in order to provide us with advance notice of coming atrocities.

John stated that the first time machine will be invented by GE in 2034. The device will be seized by the Military shortly thereafter on a must have basis.

The biggest thing he discussed was an American Civil war which would start in 2004 and escalate into Word War 3 by 2015. The civil war never took place and critics went on the attack by demanding to know why the prediction had not come true.

In the event John Titor was who and what he said, those responsible for starting the unrest may have read his posts and either delayed or abandoned their plans all together.

John stated that while on this time line he stayed in the state of Florida with his parents and his two year old self. There are those who say that while time travelling you should never encounter a younger version of yourself due to the possibility of paradoxes.

John spoke of the many-worlds theory and said that meeting yourself did not change anything on your original time line.

John supposedly returned to 2036 and his Mother contacted an attorney who in turn contacted another attorney by the name of Larry Haber. Larry Haber is an entertainment attorney who works for Disney. This created a lot of criticism because it gave the notion that the story must have been meant for entertainment.

I will defend the John Titor story by stating that the choice of a family attorney does not determine the legitimacy of the case.

The most damaging argument that I found against John's story is where someone has stated that the URL used to do the posts can be traced back to Larry Haber and/or his brother. The questions are, did the attorney hired by John's Mother contact Larry before or after John returned to the future and did John communicate with Larry at any time?

The way I answer this question is with a scenario. Lets say that a time traveler comes from the future and asked you to set up a URL so that they could post an the internet and you oblige them.

The time traveler returns to their original time line and you proceed to broadcast the story only to have someone trace the URL to you, there you stand, as they say, with egg on your face and a confused grin.

In the event Larry Haber did set up the URL for John then he should have pointed out that he had done so and provided his public with the entire story to begin with.

The fact that the John Titor foundation is on Disney Land is another flaw which should and could have been avoided by purchasing or renting office space in the general public.

According to John's web page the machine works within the structure of an automobile. There were critics who argued that this was a reference to the 1985 movie, *Back to the Future*.

The way I look at it, if someone invents a time machine that works with an automobile the fact that there was a movie made regarding the very subject prior to the invention of the device should not cause one to question the inventor's creditability.

There have been several scientists and physicists who have gone over the story with a fine tooth comb and are unable to find anything in theory that indicates a hoax.

I am convinced that the real reason people call the John Titor story a hoax is because John did not take his machine to their offices and provide a demonstration.

I am comfortable that I have provided sufficient scientific argument concerning Time Travel. I have given you the science and pseudoscience of a subject that I believe is possible and will one day be accomplished.

There are a great many people today who feel that everything that can be invented and discovered has already been invented and discovered. They look back across history and celebrate what they believe to be all that exists and ever will exist.

I look back across history and celebrate the accomplishments of great scientists and physicists and look to the future and dream of future accomplishments.

Legal

There are legal questions surrounding Time Travel and I am not afraid to address them. I will be honest though; my legal advice is worth no more than the satisfaction you find in reading it.

I do not have a law degree and the twelve and one half years that I have worked in security do not certify me as an attorney.

I have always heard people say that if you invented a time machine and the government found out about it then they would certainly remove it from your possession. I have absolutely no doubt that there is an abundance of truth to that statement.

I do not want to sound like someone who does not trust the government because I have never had any bad experiences with Law Enforcement and do not plan to create any.

The only logic that I can see in a legal ban on time machines would be due to the fear people have of paradoxes and the ripple effects of a sudden intervention with some past event.

In the event you travelled back in time and found yourself

at Ford's theatre on the night of 14 April 1865, would you be legally obligated to provide advance warning to Abraham Lincoln or some member of his security detail?

I am certain that you would feel an urge to step forward and stop this terrible catastrophe that left an entire nation in mourning; I know that I would regardless of whatever paradox or ripple effect that it might cause.

There is no doubt that once the scene unfolds as it originally did you would not announce that you knew all along what was going to happen and start naming those who were eventually apprehended as conspirators.

I could understand the legal system of 1865 considering you an accessory due to the fact that you stepped into their presence with advance knowledge of a political assassination and done absolutely nothing to prevent it from taking place.

The fact you are there to observe this incident does little for your defense and makes you appear sadistic.

There would no doubt be a different interpretation of the law when you returned to your original time line. The authorities, in the here and now, would be appreciative of your decision not to interfere with the original script.

I cannot say for sure that I would even broadcast my experience. I know that most people would demand proof and in the event the time traveler is unwilling to provide that proof they would for certain be accused of fabricating the story.

In the event you cater to the whims of the skeptical and demonstrate how the device works you can rest assured that it will sooner or later be taken from you.

The legal questions concerning Time Travel are numerous and what I have covered is just one.

I hope that physical human Time Travel will one day be possible and that the ability to practice it will be unrestricted. In the event I am not around to enjoy the process perhaps someone will read this book and come back to get me.

In the mean time I would like to advise anyone who

has the ability to travel in time to protect your machine and keep it serviced. There is a saying that I often see on bumper stickers, *Drive It like You Stole It.* The best way to avoid legal confiscation of your device is simply not to let anyone know that you have it.

Religious

The religious questions surrounding whether or not a human being can travel in time are the reasons I decided to write this book.

I became a Born-Again Christian in the fourth grade and basically grew up in church. I accept the Bible to be the full and complete word of Almighty God.

I believe that human life began, as it says in Genesis, in the Garden of Eden and I believe that the earth and all life will end the way it says in Revelation.

I do believe that time is a straight line but I believe that you can move back and forth on that line. I also believe that there are other time lines which run parallel to the one we live on and I will address that as we progress.

There are various opinions on the subject. If two people come to the same overall conclusion they still experience diversity concerning issues such as, can you change the past? I personally do not believe that God would allow you to change anything but he may allow you to be there and observe it first hand.

In the course of my study I read several commentaries that were written by Christians. I found every one of them informative and though based on scripture they were written to accommodate the opinions of the author.

I believe that physical human Time Travel is possible so therefore my writings will reflect my belief.

In answering those who attempt to tell me what God

thinks and how he will deal with things I am reminded of the following scripture.

> For my thoughts *are* not your thoughts, neither
> *are* your ways my ways, saith the Lord.
> Isaiah 55:8
> KJV 1611

There is no scripture in the Bible that says man *can* travel in time and none that says he *can't*.

I realize that certain passages can be and have been taken out of context by those who want to prove their theory.

I have done the best I can to locate the misinterpretations and reveal them to you. I respect every man's opinion and I know how it feels to be attacked when opinions differ and causes seem threatened.

I decided to conduct my research by reading commentaries and articles written by those who are attempting to debunk the notion of Time Travel.

I have recorded and researched the scriptures that were used in these works and have no trouble addressing them here because I am certain that they do not mean that man cannot travel in time.

I mentioned this in part one and I will mention it again because it is the most important scripture in the Bible when determining proper interpretation.

> Study to shew thyself approved unto God, a
> workman that needeth not to be ashamed,
> rightly dividing the word of truth.
> 2 Timothy 2:15
> KJV 1611

I mentioned another verse in part 1 that I feel should be mentioned here also and that is the following scripture.

"Neither give heed to fables and endless
genealogies, which minister questions, rather
than godly edifying which is in faith: *so do*".
1 Timothy 1:4
KJV 1611

I want to make it clear before I go any further that I do
not intend to minister questions but to answer them. I do not
deny the fact that there are questions because if there were no
questions this work would not exist.

I am attempting to prove the possibility of Time Travel so
therefore I claim the following scripture.

For with God nothing shall be impossible.
Luke 1:37
KJV 1611

Luke 1:37 is a statement made to Mary by the angel during
their conversation concerning the Immaculate Conception and
Virgin Birth of Christ Jesus.

I acknowledge without hesitation that it is not talking
about Time Travel. I will say however that when the angel said
nothing shall be impossible he did not add, *with the exception
of travelling in time.*

Several years ago in Greenbelt, Maryland, scientists were
doing some research into what the position of the sun, moon
and planets would be over the next 100 to 1000 years. We
need this information in order to prevent our satellites from
bumping into unexpected objects.

They ran the tests over past centuries only to have the
equipment run into what I will refer to as technological
confusion.

The machine indicated that there was a missing day
somewhere in history. The scientists were spell bound until

one man who was a Christian spoke up and said that there was scripture in the Bible which proved the findings. There was skepticism but they were all willing to entertain a study.

The first scripture they reviewed was Joshua 10:1-15 where it records how God made the sun and the moon stand still while Israel conquered their enemies.

The following tests indicated that this had in fact occurred for a total of twenty-three hours and twenty minutes. Where was the remaining forty minutes?

The answer was found in Isaiah 38:7-8 where God made the sun go back ten degrees as a sign to King Hezekiah that his life would be prolonged fifteen years. NASA determined that ten degrees was forty minutes.

I am certain that numerous people world wide passed away during that twenty-four hour period but they were not brought back to life. Time lost an entire day yet nothing changed.

I mentioned all of that because it indicates a form of Time Travel that has already been accomplished and in Biblical proportions none the less.

With that said let's begin reviewing scripture.

Wherefore I perceive that *there* is nothing better, than that a man should rejoice in his own works; for that is his portion: for who shall bring him to see what shall be after him?
Ecclesiastes 3:22
KJV 1611

This is one of the verses that I found in anti Time Travel commentaries due to the fact that it asks who shall bring a man to see what shall come after him.

The answer to this question as pertains to Time Travel is simple. In the event you build a time machine and go three hundred years into the future and upon your arrival perform a search into your own history all you will find is a missing persons report.

You departed your original time line, someone came looking for you and you were not there. Time moved at the normal speed for them while you instantly skipped over the next three hundred years.

Ecclesiastes 3:22 means that a man cannot see what his future or the future concerning him holds. It does not debunk the possibility of Time Travel.

I also discovered the following scripture being used to debunk Time Travel.

> Because to every purpose there is time and
> judgment, therefore the misery of man *is* great
> upon him. For he knoweth not that which shall
> be: for who can tell him when it shall be?
> Ecclesiastes 8:6-7
> KJV 1611

This scripture brings up the one fact that many people do not like. There is a purpose to everything that takes place and God is no respecter of persons, therefore he will not interfere with certain occurrences because they are part of his overall plan.

I have been asked during discussions on the matter if a time traveler could go into the future and find out when the rapture will happen and the answer is no.

> But of that day and hour knoweth no *man*, no,
> not the angels of heaven, but my Father only.
> Matthew 24:36
> KJV 1611

The one thing that must be kept in mind is that nothing happens unless God allows it to happen. God would never allow a human being to discover that information to begin with.

This is the perfect place for me to address the one overall

question that many people, especially Christians, have: whether we can discover what will happen in the future.

I mentioned John Titor and how that he claimed to have been a time traveler from 2036. I covered the statement he made about America entering into a civil war in 2004 and that this would escalate into World War 3 by 2015. John was telling us what would happen in the future and in the event he was who and what he said his interaction created a paradox because the civil war did not take place.

I believe that the best way to answer the question is to clarify past, present and future. If John Titor really was a time traveler he was telling us his past because he had already lived through it.

John's past would be our future so therefore Time Travel critics would say that revealing the information violates the scripture because it leaves us knowing the future.

The civil war never occurred so we obviously did not know the future. In the event it was something that was to actually come about John's interaction created a paradox or as opposed to changing the past this was part of the plan of time.

I realize that my answer seems contradictory by saying that we cannot change the past and then indicating that the change was part of the overall plan.

I will point out the many-worlds theory at this point and proceed to answer another question I'm sure you have. *If there are multiple universes and people travelling in time, what happens with those universes and time travelers at the moment of the rapture?*

The answer I provide may not please the critics because any answer to any question they pose is never appreciated, however; the answer is SUCTION.

The very moment Jesus Christ places his feet in the clouds and the rapture of the church occurs all time lines and time travelers will be called into headquarters.

I must return to Ecclesiastes 8:6-7 and point out that there is a time and a judgment to every purpose so perhaps John Titor's arrival on our time line was for a purpose.

I used the illustration of a time traveler finding themselves at Ford's Theatre on the night of 14 April 1865 just minutes prior to President Lincoln's assassination. The question I posed was whether or not you had an obligation to provide advance warning.

I am certain that no matter how persuasive and well meaning you are there is no way President Lincoln or his security detail would take the information seriously. *Or would they?* I believe there is scripture to show that God will allow only the outcome he wants.

> For the scripture saith unto Pharaoh, Even for this same purpose have I raised thee up, that I might shew my power in thee, and that my name might be declared throughout all the earth.
> Romans 9:17
> KJV1611

Romans 9:17 is in reference to the events in the Biblical book of Exodus, Chapters 7-12 when God sent Moses before the Pharaoh to ask for the freedom of the Israelites.

Exodus 7:1-5 details God's conversation with Moses concerning what to say when he approached Pharaoh.

God makes it clear that he will harden Pharaoh's heart so that he will not hearken, thus providing God the opportunity to lay his hand upon Egypt and reveal his power.

God sent ten plagues upon Egypt. Each time Moses made the same request and each time God hardened Pharaoh's heart so that he would refuse the request.

The ten plagues were – *Water turned to blood, Frogs, Lice, Wild Animals, Disease on Livestock, Boils on the Skin, Hail and Thunder, Locusts, Darkness, and Death of the First Born.*

Following these ten plagues God softened the heart of Pharaoh and the Children of Israel were released.

I am sure that you are wondering by now what all of that

has to do with whether or not Abraham Lincoln would heed the words of a time traveler who provides advance warning of his unfortunate fate.

I have two points to make and both are intended with the deepest respect for our sixteenth President.

The first point I want to make is that Lincoln's Presidency was ordained by God for the purpose of delivering the slaves from their bondage. Lincoln was an American Moses.

The second point I want to make is that you cannot change history no matter how hard you try. *Or can you?*

God may allow you to travel back to 1865 and have a detailed conversation with Abraham Lincoln, however; God will not allow the President to heed your warnings. *Or will he?*

I have also been asked the question, what if Lincoln had you arrested and jailed for being a spy or just plain harassment?

These questions falls into the paradox category and can be answered with the same philosophy on which the entire scenario is based. God ordains all things for a purpose and as opposed to being a set back it is simply part of the script.

I mentioned the many-worlds theory of parallel universes and how that when you Time Travel you may end up on a totally different time line where things, though altered, do not effect where you come from.

I was once asked a question concerning what would happen if you travelled back in time to interact with someone who is now deceased and brought them to your time line. The concept is the fact that this individual has already departed their physical dwelling and is now in the presence of Almighty God.

The soul is with the Lord when you depart your time line and is still with him when you arrive in the past. In the event you bring them to your time line there will be two versions of the same soul, one with the Lord and one in the physical body before your eyes. This works the same way as meeting a younger or older version of you while time travelling.

I believe that God knows in advance what will happen

and he will always redeem shed blood and tears for better tomorrows. President Lincoln's assassination was a painful experience for America and our time line. Despite the fact everyone who remembered it is now deceased there is and always will be pain associated with that awful event in history, especially among the African American race who owes their freedom to his last great act, *The Emancipation Proclamation*.

I look back over history and I see other occurrences to which I feel there must have been more pleasant multiple choice endings.

The assassination of President John F. Kennedy no doubt changed world history. President Kennedy did not want to take America into the Vietnam conflict and just days prior to his death had approved the assassination of communist North Vietnam's President.

In the event this plan had been executed North Vietnam would have fallen under non-communist leadership and perhaps thousands of lives could have been spared.

Robert F. Kennedy was running for President on a platform of ending the war in Vietnam when he was senselessly murdered in the kitchen of the Ambassador Hotel in Las Angeles, California on 5 June 1968.

One author stated that every time he reads the names on the Vietnam Memorial in Washington, D.C. he has to pause for the names of those who died after 20 January 1969, the day Robert Kennedy might have been inaugurated as the thirty-seventh President of the United States and question how much shorter the wall may have been had this tragic assassination not taken place.

The assassination of Dr. Martin Luther King, Jr. was one occurrence that defiantly changed the course of history.

I personally believe that by 1970 Dr. King's civil rights dream would have been realized and he would have stepped into another role. One can only assume, however; I am certain that Dr. King would have become an anti-drug crusader.

I think of the introduction of the drug culture in the 1970s coupled with the rise of heavy metal music through which so many young people were influenced to experiment with illegal mind altering chemicals and Satanism.

I feel that under the influence of men like JFK, RFK and MLK there would have been different outcomes throughout the decade of the seventies and even into the eighties.

There were people who lived during the years these men were in leadership positions and were influenced to take stands for which they are remembered and celebrated today.

If these men's influence changed destinies while they were alive then destinies were changed by their deaths and destinies would have been changed in the years to follow had they not been assassinated.

The destinies that may have been changed over the next two decades could have been those of America's most notorious serial killers, bank robbers, and child molesters.

There is also no way to tell how many people turned to drugs and alcohol as a result of the pain caused by these men's deaths.

I realize that most of what I have related to you concerning the history of political assassination and the paradox possibilities is more philosophical than religious, however; I feel that it all fits together like a hand in a glove.

The overall will of God and man's free will never fails to crash into one another and the results are like that of a kitten attempting to dethrone a lion as king of the jungle.

There are many scriptures which deal with time and despite man's concept of the subject. Here is a couple.

But, beloved, be not ignorant of this one thing,
that one day *is* with the Lord as a thousand
years, and a thousand years as one day.
2 Peter 3:8
KJV 1611

According as he hath chosen us in him before
the foundation of the world, that we should be
holy and without blame before him in love.
Ephesians 1:4
KJV 1611

These two verses show that God is an eternal being who
not only created everything but can see the future as if it were
the past.

These are Biblical references to time and they are to be
taken seriously and not doubted or made fun.

I ended part one by providing the reader with God's one
and only plan of Salvation and I will end part two on the same
note since there are some who will read only the section that
applies to their interests.

The Bible plainly tells us what God done in order to
provide a way for the human race to be saved.

For God so loved the world, that he gave his only
begotten son, that whosoever believeth in him
should not perish, but have everlasting life.
John 3:16
KJV 1611

What is the method?

For by grace are ye saved through faith; and
that not of yourselves: *it is* the gift of God.
Ephesians 2:8
KJV 1611

Who needs a Savior?

For all have sinned and come short of the glory of God.
Romans 3:23
KJV 1611

Who can save us?

Neither is there salvation in any other: for
there is none other name given under heaven
among men, whereby we must be saved.
Acts 4:12
KJV 1611

How are we saved?

That if thou shalt confess with thy mouth the Lord
Jesus, and shalt believe in thine heart that God hath
raised him from the dead, thou shalt be saved.
Romans 10:9
KJV 1611

These verses are a road map to becoming a Born-Again Christian. There are multiple religions in the world but only one way to know for certain that we will be with our creator for all of eternity.

The plan of salvation is as simple as ABC.

1 – ADMIT – That you are a sinner – Romans 3:23

2 – BELIEVE – That Jesus Christ is the only way of salvation – Acts 4:12

3 – CONFESS – Jesus Christ as Lord – Romans 10:9

I would not have accomplished my goal unless I provided you with what is commonly referred to as the sinner's prayer. In the event you would like to be saved simply pray the following prayer.

Heavenly Father, I admit that I am a sinner. I believe that you sent your only begotten son in order to provide a way for me to be saved. I believe that he suffered and died and that you raised him from the dead. I confess with my mouth that Jesus Christ is the only name given under heaven among men whereby we must be saved. Lord Jesus, please forgive me of my sins, come into my heart and be my savior. I make you the Lord of my life. In Jesus name I pray, Amen.

In the event you prayed this prayer and meant it in your heart you were just adopted into the family of Almighty God. You are now one of his children and a brother or sister to every Christian who ever was, is or ever will be.

I never set out to make someone believe that time travel is possible unless they already believed that it was. The one overall goal of this work is to lift up Christianity and bring as many souls as possible to a saving knowledge of Jesus Christ.

There are those who will read what I have written and dismiss it while there are those who will absorb and accept it with an open mind and heart. These are the ones I want to hear from.

In the event you have accepted Jesus Christ as a result of reading my work I want to hear from you. I can be reached at *BookOnUniversalAuthority@gmail.com*. I cannot promise a response to everyone but just the joy of knowing that I was successful will make my day.

Conclusion

I trust that you have enjoyed reading *Universal Authority* as much as I have enjoyed writing it.

There is so much more that I could address concerning these subjects, however; for the sake of length and time I will keep my arguments short and to the point. I read a statement by one author who said that he wrote short books to give people something they do not get often and that is the pleasure of completion.

I did not set out to make people believe in the existence of Extra-Terrestrial Intelligence and Time Travel unless they already did. In the event they already held these beliefs I trust that I have provided them with a new overall outlook.

I conducted my research by looking for answers to the critic's questions. I considered everything that has been posed to me over the years and sought to prove that it was either irrelevant or unrelated to the subject. I am certain that I have accomplished my goal.

There is no doubt that scientifically Extra-Terrestrial intelligence and Time Travel are possible. I have covered this area by addressing NASA, SETI and the work of numerous scientists and physicists who have devoted their lives to research and inventions that have profoundly and dramatically affected and changed not only our lives but the world we live in.

There are also more than a few questions concerning the legal ramifications of interaction with a race from another world and travelling through time. I covered this area by providing scenarios based on historical events and what your responsibilities would or would not be as well as what paradoxes could spring off of your decision to intervene with original occurrences.

The most difficult yet interesting questions to tackle were those pertaining to religion. I became a Born-Again Christian in grade school and have always accepted the Bible to be the inspired word of Almighty God; therefore I found this area to be my overall calling and placed the most emphasis on it.

The one question that comes up in Extra-Terrestrial discussion most often is, if there is life anywhere besides earth then who is their Savior because Jesus was crucified for earth? Did Jesus incarnate in other forms on other planets and die for those beings also? The truth is, Jesus incarnated, died and resurrected one time for the human soul and it does not matter where the human soul is, they can be saved as a result of that one act.

The fact that sin started on earth in the Garden of Eden does not bind sin to the earth because at the moment the human race fell, that sin overtook all of creation.

In the beginning God created the heavens and the earth. And the earth was without form, and void; and darkness was upon the face of the deep. And the Spirit of God moved upon the face of the waters.

The earth was without form, and void. I do not see where the heavens were without form, and void.

I was once asked, if time travel is possible could someone travel back to the days of Jesus and walk with the Savior? The answer is no, because we are commanded to accept the works of Christ by faith and travelling back to witness them first hand would remove the need for faith.

I believe in the possibility of Extra-Terrestrial Existence and Time Travel with a passion.

I know in my heart that our Creator is Almighty, All Powerful and All Knowing. I know that He is in control and everything that happens serves a purpose.

In the event God wants us to communicate with other worldly beings and/or travel in time then he will make the arrangements.

Christians have a great travel planner; one day when Jesus puts his feet in the clouds and the Angel Gabriel blows his trumpet, we are going to take the trip of a life time. I am speaking of the rapture of the Church.

Christians look forward to the rapture because it means the end of pain and suffering for those of us who know Christ in a personal way. I also look forward to that day for the same reasons, however; the sad thing about the rapture is that it means the end of precious opportunities to accept what the Savior has done for us.

The truth is *Universal Authority* was not my first idea for a book and I almost didn't write it.

I have an incredible interest in politics and found tremendous inspiration in a statement that President Kennedy made in his inaugural. – *"and to remember that, in the past, those who foolishly sought power by riding the back of the tiger ended up inside."*

President Kennedy was referencing communism and I was referencing the American political system.

I had researched the issues from the 2008 presidential election and came up with fifteen of my own. I compiled everything into platform style and titled it *Leading The Tiger*.

I wanted to provide the reader with my ideas for what it would take to bring America out of debt, end the wars we find ourselves in and restore the world's perception of us. I wanted to point out that too many elected officials have acquired their positions by riding the back of the tiger.

I began the manuscript only to realize that I was in fact riding and not leading the tiger. I was addressing political issues because I felt that doing so would provide me with more creditability as an author than writing on the issues closest to my heart.

I am thankful for the fact that God opened my eyes and delivered me from that terrible misconception. I am grateful for strength, courage and completed work.

I wrote *Universal Authority* not because I wanted to acquire fame and fortune but because I have a desire to see people come to Jesus Christ.

I am not saying that *Leading The Tiger* will not manifest in the future, I am only saying that the timing was not appropriate. I needed to set the tone with my true feelings and let the world know who I really am.

I found inspiration in the words of several statements that I discovered during the course of my research and I want to share a few of them here.

> You don't write because you want to say something;
> you write because you have something to say.
> F. Scott Fitzgerald

> Better to write for yourself and have no public,
> than to write for the public and have no self.
> Cyril Connolly

These two pertain to the strength that it took for me to lay aside all of the personal pursuits of fame and fortune and provide the findings of my research into Extra-Terrestrial Intelligence and Time Travel.

I still felt, as many authors do, a fear of rejection and began to look for some words of comfort, preferably from someone who had already made a stand on something for which they will always be remembered.

I found the following statement with which I will leave you and I hope that everyone who comes to this work will come away with this as their motto.

I would rather lose in a cause that will some day win, than win in a cause that will some day lose.
Woodrow Wilson

Acknowledgements

There are so many people who have been influential in my life and who have assisted me in becoming the person I am today.

I acknowledge both of my parents to whom this work is dedicated. My Father passed away when I was six years old so I never really got to know him yet through his demons of alcohol and hard feelings I was influenced to avoid all mind altering chemicals. *Dad, thanks for the lessons, I love and miss you.*

I mentioned that despite the passage of thirty-one years I can still recall that day and I recall the care, concern and dedication that my Mother poured into my upbringing and education. *Mom, Thanks for both provision and pampering, I love and miss you.*

I acknowledge all of my family whose constant presence and support have kept me on track over the years. *Thanks for keeping in touch.*

I acknowledge the blessing of being raised in church where I was taught the word of God and how that hiding its words in my heart would always direct my foot steps in the right direction.

I acknowledge all of the individuals with whom I attended

church and whose words and/or interaction have been a blessing to me. *You are the reason I turned out the way I did.*

I acknowledge every single teacher and school official with whom I had contact during the years of my education. In the event there is something I should know that I do not then it is my fault for failing to pay attention. *God knows you done the best you could.*

I acknowledge the Washington County Virginia Public Library main branch in Abingdon, Virginia where I conducted my research and whose supply of information and word processors made this work possible. *You folks are wonderful.*

I acknowledge my good friend Charlie Fugate who assisted me more than once with proof reading and final submission. *Thanks Bro.*

I acknowledge the great people at *iUniverse Publishing* for the superb job they have done at placing my work before the public and for keeping in touch and listening to my many ideas for a book before I finally settled on a subject. *May others learn from you.*

I acknowledge every single individual whose path and mine have ever crossed. In the event you were my friend and nice to me your words and friendship has been a blessing. In the event you were mean to me and we failed to click then rest assured that the infuriation which followed also played a positive part in where I am today. *My interaction with you has been beneficial whether as a reward or a test.*

I issue a very special acknowledgement to my very special friend Alexis Rogers of Phoenix, Arizona with whom I have shared the last one and a half year of my life through U.S. mail and telephone correspondence. *Sweetheart, your friendship and understanding are the reasons this work exists and we will be together soon.*

References

Part 1

1 – http://www.quotationspage.com/quotes/Sam_Ewing

2 – http://www.policyalmanac.org/economic/archive/nasa_history.shtml

3 – http://netmillionairesclub.ning.com/forum/topics/fun-quotes-that-did-not-turn

4 – http://www.seti.org/page.aspx?pid=572

5 – http://planetary.org/explore/topics/seti/seti_history_02.html

6 – http://www.seti.org/

7 – http://www.newmexico.org/experience/unusual_unique/roswell.php

8 – http://www.unmuseum.org/germufo.htm

9 – http://en.wikipedia.org/wiki/Roswell_UFO_incident

10 – http://www.wpafb.af.mil/

11 – http://lithiumdreamer.tripod.com/ufoart.html

12 – http://ufoevidence.org/cases/case487.htm

13 – http://www.X-PPAC.org/

14 – http://www.gly.uga.edu/railsback/1122science2.html

15 – http://en.wikipedia.org/wiki/wow!_signal

16 – http://www.bibliotecapleyades.net/exopolitics/esp_
exopolitics_Q_O.html

17 – http://en.wikipedia.org/wiki/Exotheology

18 – http://www.geocentricity.com/ba1/no112/spacetravel.
pdf

19 – http://en.wikipedia.org/wiki/Anunnaki

20 – http://www.arlev.co.uk/zechhome.htm

21 – http://en.wikipedia.org/wiki/moon_Landing#Manned_
landings

22 – Blum, Howard. Out There. New York: Simon and
Schuster, 1990

23 – Holy Bible KJV 1611

Part 2

1 – http://www.quotationspage.com/quote/28981.html

2 – http://en.wikipedia.org/wiki/Benjamin_Franklin

3 – http://en.wikipedia.org/wiki/Alexander_Graham_Bell

4 – http://en.wikipedia.org/Elisha_Gray

5 – http://en.wikipedia.org/wiki/Elliot_Cresson_Medal

6 – http://www.2.fi.edu/

7 – http://en.wikipedia.org/wiki/Allesandro_Volta

8 – http://en.wikipedia.org/wiki/Georg_Ohm

9 – http://en.wikipedia.org/wiki/Thomas_Edison

10 – http://en.wikipedia.org/wiki/Nikola_Tesla

11 – http://en.wikipedia.org/wiki/Philadelphia_Experiment

12 – http://en.wikipedia.org/wiki/Albert_Einstein

13 – http://en.wikipedia.org/wiki/Unified_field_theory

14 – http://en.wikipedia.org/wiki/USS_Eldridge_(DE-173)

15 – http://en.wikipedia.org/wiki/Time_travel

16 – http://en.wikipedia.org/wiki/Ronald_Mallett

17 – http://en.wikipedia.org/wiki/The_Time_Machine

18 – http://newsok.com/harvey-firestone/article/3403355

19 – http://www.designprobe.com/trends/watch.html

20 – http://en.wikipedia.org/wiki/Wright_brothers

21 – http://en.wikipedia.org/wiki/Special_relativity

22 – http://en.wikipdia.org/wiki/Galileo_Galilei

23 – http://en.wikipedia.org/wiki/Black_hole

24 – http://en.wikipedia.org/wiki/White_hole

25 – http://en.wikipedia.org/wiki/wormhole

26 – http://en.wikipedia.org/wiki/Stephen_Hawking

27 – http://www.trutv.com/conspiracy/government-lies/time-travel/philadelphia-experiment.html

28 – http://en.wikipedia.org/wiki/Psuedoscience

29 – http://en.wikipedia.org/wiki/Hugh_Everett_III

30 – http://en.wikipedia.org/wiki/Many_worlds_interpretation

31 – http://en.wikipeia.org/wiki/John_Titor

32 – http://www.johntitor.com/

33 – http://www.snopes.com/religion/lostday.asp

34 – http://en.wikipedia.org/wiki/Abraham_Lincoln

35 – http://en.wikipedia.org/wiki/Emancipation_
   Proclamation

36 – Randles, Jenny. Breaking The Time Barrier. New York:
   Paraview, 2005

37 – Mallett, Ronald L. and Bruce Henderson. Time
   Traveler: A Scientist's Personal Mission to make Time
   Travel a Reality New York: Thunder's Mouth, 2006

38 – Zukav, Gary. The Dancing Wu Li Masters: An
   Overview of the New Physics. New York: Harper
   Collins, 1979

39 – Gott, Richard J. Time Travel In Einstein's Universe.
   New York: Houghton Mifflin, 2001

40 – Holy Bible KJV 1611